Money Matters 101 - Financial Planning Essentials

While every precaution has been taken in the preparation of this book, the publisher assumes no responsibility for errors or omissions, or for damages resulting from the use of the information contained herein.

Money Matters 101 - Financial Planning Essentials
First edition. April 1, 2024.

Written by Drishti Sapra.

Table of Contents

1.1   Setting Financial Goals

1.1.1 Define the importance of setting specific, measurable, achievable, relevant, and time-bound (SMART) financial goals

In today's fast-paced world, financial planning has transcended beyond mere saving. It's about strategizing, aiming for tangible achievements, and setting oneself up for long-term prosperity. Herein lies the quintessence of SMART—Specific, Measurable, Achievable, Relevant, and Time-bound—financial goals. Imagine you're embarking on a treasure hunt, where the map is your financial plan and the treasure is your financial independence. Without a clear route or checkpoints, how likely are you to find the treasure? This analogy underscores the critical nature of SMART financial goals. They are not just about reaching a destination but enjoying a journey marked by growth, security, and eventual success.

- ❖ **Specific**: The importance of specificity cannot be overstated. It's the difference between saying "I want to save money" and "I want to save $10,000 for a down payment on a house in two years." This clarity directs your efforts and resources efficiently.

- ❖ **Measurable**: Setting measurable goals means your progress can be quantified. This could involve tracking your savings monthly to ensure you're on track to accumulate that $10,000. Without measurability, assessing progress becomes subjective and demotivating.

- ❖ **Achievable**: Goals need to be realistic. Setting the bar too high can lead to frustration and abandonment. If your goal is to save $10,000 in two years, you need to assess your income and expenses to ensure it's feasible.

- ❖ **Relevant**: Relevance ensures your goals align with your values and long-term objectives. Saving for a house because it's a stepping stone to building wealth for your family makes the goal not only relevant but also motivational.

- ❖ **Time-bound**: A deadline acts as a powerful motivator. Knowing you have two years to save for the house instills a sense of urgency and focus. Time-bound goals help prioritize actions and resources.

Let's illustrate with an example: Jane, a graphic designer, aims to transition to freelance work. Her SMART goal is to save $15,000 for living expenses over the next year to comfortably make the switch. This goal is specific (saving $15,000), measurable (tracking monthly savings), achievable (based on her income and spending), relevant (facilitates her career transition), and time-bound (one-year deadline).

The beauty of SMART financial goals lies in their simplicity and effectiveness. They compel us to articulate what we truly desire, chart a clear path toward achieving it, and hold ourselves accountable. In a world brimming with uncertainties, having a well-defined financial roadmap not only brings peace of mind but also empowers us to navigate through life's financial challenges with confidence. Start setting your SMART financial goals today, and watch as your financial dreams transform into achievable realities.

1.1.2 Examples of Short-Term and Long-Term Financial Goals

Embarking on a financial journey without a map can feel like navigating a ship in uncharted waters—overwhelming, directionless, and fraught with uncertainty. Whether you're a fresh graduate stepping into the real world, a mid-career professional aiming for financial stability, or nearing retirement, setting clear financial goals is the compass that guides your ship to the harbor of financial freedom. Distinguishing between short-term and long-term financial goals not only helps in prioritizing your financial activities but also in achieving a balanced and fulfilling life. Let's delve into the realm of financial planning with tangible examples of short-term and long-term goals, paving the way for a future you can look forward to with confidence.

- ❖ **Short-Term Financial Goals:** These are your immediate to two-year milestones, crucial for daily financial stability and laying the groundwork for your future ambitions.
  - ➢ **Creating an Emergency Fund:** An essential cushion of three to six months' worth of living expenses to protect against unforeseen events.
  - ➢ **Paying Off Credit Card Debt:** High-interest debt can be a drain on your resources. Targeting this debt aggressively is a smart financial move.
  - ➢ **Saving for a Vacation:** Rather than incurring debt for leisure, saving for a trip enhances the experience by eliminating financial stress.

- ➢ **Starting an Investment Fund:** Even a small amount set aside regularly can introduce you to the world of investing without overwhelming commitment.

- ❖ **Long-Term Financial Goals:** These goals span several years or decades, focusing on substantial achievements and life milestones.
    - ➢ **Purchasing a Home:** Saving for a down payment on a house is a common long-term goal, requiring discipline and a strategic savings plan.
    - ➢ **Funding Your Child's Education:** A 529 Plan or an education savings account can be a proactive way to ensure your child's college expenses are covered.
    - ➢ **Retirement Planning:** Consistently contributing to a retirement account, like a 401(k) or an IRA, can ensure a comfortable and secure retirement.
    - ➢ **Paying Off Your Mortgage:** While it's a long-term commitment, the peace of mind and financial freedom that come from owning your home outright are unparalleled.

Setting both short-term and long-term financial goals is akin to plotting waypoints on your journey to financial success. While short-term goals focus on securing your financial footing, long-term goals aim at achieving your dream lifestyle and ensuring security in your golden years. Remember, the clarity of your goals determines the effectiveness of your financial plan. By taking the time to define these goals clearly, you're not just planning for financial success; you're architecting a life filled with achievement, stability, and peace of mind. Start today, and transform your financial dreams into achievable realities, one goal at a time.

1.1.3 How to Prioritize Goals Based on Their Importance and Urgency

In the bustling crossroads of life, where personal ambitions intersect with professional deadlines, the art of prioritizing goals becomes the guiding star. Imagine your goals as a myriad of stars in the night sky. While all may twinkle, only a few guide you to your destination. In a world brimming with opportunities and challenges, understanding how to prioritize your goals by their importance and urgency is not just a skill—it's a necessity. This navigational prowess ensures that you invest your time, energy, and resources into endeavors that propel you toward your aspirations efficiently and effectively. Let's embark on a journey to master this crucial skill, ensuring that you can distinguish the North Star of your goals amidst a sky full of demands.

- ❖ **Understanding Importance vs. Urgency:** First, decipher the difference between what's important and what's urgent. Important activities are those that contribute to your long-term mission, values, and goals. In contrast, urgent activities demand immediate attention and are often associated with achieving someone else's goals. The Eisenhower Box, a simple yet powerful tool, can help classify your tasks into four categories: important and urgent, important but not urgent, not important but urgent, and not important and not urgent.
- ❖ **Strategies for Prioritization:**
  - ➢ **Eisenhower Box (Matrix):** Use this matrix to categorize tasks. Focus on completing tasks that are both important and urgent first, plan for important but not urgent tasks, delegate the not important but urgent tasks, and eliminate those that are neither important nor urgent.

- ➢ **Setting SMART Goals:** Ensure your goals are Specific, Measurable, Achievable, Relevant, and Time-bound. This clarity will help in recognizing which goals are important and warrant priority.
- ➢ **The 80/20 Rule (Pareto Principle):** Often, 20% of your efforts produce 80% of the results. Identify and prioritize these high-impact activities.
- ➢ **Daily To-Do Lists:** Start each day with a list of tasks ranked by their importance and urgency. This daily practice keeps you focused and productive.

- ❖ **Applying Prioritization in Real Life:**
Consider Anna, a project manager juggling professional development, leading a team project, and personal fitness goals. By applying the Eisenhower Box, she identifies her certification study (important and urgent) and team project deadlines (important but urgent) as top priorities. Fitness, while important, falls into the important but not urgent category, prompting her to schedule regular, though not immediate, workout sessions.

Prioritizing goals by their importance and urgency is akin to navigating through a dense fog with a reliable compass. It's about making informed choices that align with your core values and long-term vision. By mastering this skill, you not only enhance your efficiency and productivity but also carve a path that leads to personal and professional fulfillment. Start with the strategies outlined above, and transform the overwhelming array of stars into a clear constellation of your success.

1.1.4 Tips for Staying Motivated and Tracking Progress Toward Goals

In the marathon of life, where each stride forward is a step towards our personal and professional aspirations, maintaining motivation and tracking progress can sometimes feel like an uphill battle. The initial spark of enthusiasm often dims under the weight of routine and obstacles, leaving many to wonder how they can keep the flame alive. Whether you're aiming to climb the career ladder, improve your health, or master a new skill, the journey towards your goals is a blend of persistence, strategy, and self-reflection. Let's unlock the secrets to staying motivated and vigilantly tracking your journey towards success, ensuring that every effort counts and brings you closer to the finish line.

- ❖ **Setting Clear, Achievable Goals:**
  Begin with crystal-clear goals that are both inspiring and achievable. Use the SMART criteria to define them—Specific, Measurable, Achievable, Relevant, and Time-bound. This clarity transforms abstract desires into tangible targets.

- ❖ **Breaking Down Big Goals:**
  Large goals can be daunting. Break them down into smaller, manageable tasks to avoid feeling overwhelmed. Achieving these mini-goals can provide a regular sense of accomplishment, fueling your motivation.

- ❖ **Visual Progress Tracking:**
  Create a visual representation of your progress. This could be a progress bar, a checklist, or a journal. Visual cues act as constant reminders of how far you've come and what's left to achieve.

- ❖ **Celebrate Milestones:**
  Don't wait to reach your final goal to celebrate. Acknowledge and reward yourself for completing milestones along the way. These celebrations reinforce positive behavior and keep the motivation high.

- ❖ **Find Your 'Why':**

  Keep a vivid reminder of why you set your goals. Whether it's a photo, a motivational quote, or a written statement, let this reminder serve as a source of inspiration when the going gets tough.

- ❖ **Stay Flexible:**

  Be prepared to adjust your strategies if you encounter unexpected obstacles. Flexibility in approach can help maintain momentum even when changes occur.

- ❖ **Leverage the Power of Accountability:**

  Share your goals with a friend, family member, or a mentor who can offer support and hold you accountable. Regular check-ins can increase your sense of responsibility towards your goals.

- ❖ **Maintain a Positive Attitude:**

  Stay optimistic, even when you face setbacks. A positive mindset can enhance your resilience, enabling you to navigate through challenges more effectively.

Staying motivated and tracking progress toward your goals is a dynamic and personalized process. It's about finding what resonates with you and integrating these strategies into your daily routine. Remember, the journey towards achieving your goals is as significant as the destination itself. By celebrating small victories, embracing flexibility, and keeping your eyes on the prize, you'll not only reach your goals but also enjoy the path to getting there. Start today by applying these tips, and transform your dreams into achievable milestones on the roadmap of your life.

1.2 Creating a Budget

1.2.1 The Purpose of a Budget in Managing Finances Effectively

In the whirlwind of financial advice and myriad investment options available today, the cornerstone of personal finance remains the humble budget. Often overlooked in its simplicity, a well-crafted budget is akin to a lighthouse guiding ships safely to shore amidst a stormy sea of economic uncertainty. It's not merely about tracking expenses or limiting indulgences; it's a strategic blueprint for financial empowerment and peace of mind. Imagine embarking on a journey without a map or a clear destination. That's what navigating your financial life without a budget looks like—aimless and risky. In this topic, we will delve into the essence of budgeting, uncovering how this fundamental tool is indispensable in managing finances effectively. Through practical examples, we aim to illuminate the path to financial stability, ensuring you're well-equipped to make informed decisions that align with your long-term financial aspirations.

A Roadmap to Financial Clarity

At its core, a budget is your financial roadmap, outlining where your money comes from and where it's going. It's about understanding the difference between wants and needs and prioritizing accordingly. Consider the example of Emily, a graphic designer who found herself constantly living paycheck to paycheck. By creating a detailed budget, Emily was able to identify unnecessary expenditures, allocate funds toward her savings, and even invest in a professional course that boosted her career.

Debt Reduction and Savings Acceleration

Budgeting shines a spotlight on debt, offering strategies to eliminate it while preventing the accumulation of new financial burdens. It's about making your money work for you, not against you. John, an engineer, was able to use his budget to devise a plan that not only cleared his credit card debt but also accelerated his savings, putting him on a fast track to purchasing his first home.

Achieving Financial Goals

Whether it's saving for a dream vacation, investing in real estate, or preparing for retirement, a budget acts as a stepping stone toward your financial goals. It breaks down these ambitious objectives into manageable actions, making them more attainable. For instance, Sarah and Mark, a couple with aspirations of traveling the world, utilized their budget to systematically save a portion of their income, enabling them to explore new countries without financial stress.

Adapting to Life's Uncertainties

Life is unpredictable, but a budget offers a semblance of control. It provides a cushion for unexpected expenses, be it a medical emergency, sudden job loss, or urgent home repairs. This adaptability was crucial for Alex, who faced an unexpected medical bill. Thanks to his contingency fund, part of his budget plan, he was able to cover the expenses without derailing his financial stability.

The purpose of a budget transcends mere number crunching; it's about gaining a sense of financial freedom and security. In a world where financial uncertainty can cause significant stress and anxiety, a budget stands as a beacon of control and clarity. By embracing budgeting, you're not just managing your money; you're paving the way for a future filled with possibilities, unburdened by financial constraints. Let this tool be your ally in navigating the complexities of personal finance, transforming your dreams into achievable realities. Remember, the journey to financial success begins with a single step—a well-planned budget.

1.2.2 Step-by-Step Instructions for Creating a Budget, Including Tracking Income and Expenses

Embarking on the journey of creating a budget can feel like setting sail into uncharted financial waters. However, with the right compass and map, it transforms into an empowering voyage toward financial freedom and security. Whether you're navigating through the choppy seas of debt or cruising towards your savings goals, a well-planned budget is your most reliable navigator. In this guide, we'll walk you through the step-by-step process of crafting a budget that not only tracks your income and expenses but also steers you closer to your financial aspirations. Imagine being the captain of your ship, with a clear view of your financial horizon, making informed decisions that propel you toward your dreams. Let's set sail together and chart a course towards financial stability and growth.

Step 1: Gather Your Financial Documents

Begin your budgeting journey by collecting all your financial statements—bank statements, bills, pay stubs, and any other documents reflecting your earnings and expenditures. This step is akin to assembling all the pieces of a puzzle, providing a clear picture of your financial landscape.

Step 2: Calculate Your Total Income

Identify the total amount of income you receive each month, including salaries, bonuses, and any other sources of income. For instance, if you're like Jamie, who has a main job and a side gig as a freelance graphic designer, you'll want to add all these income streams together to get a total monthly income.

Step 3: List Your Monthly Expenses

Track every dollar you spend in a month. Categorize your expenses into fixed (rent, mortgage, insurance) and variable (groceries, entertainment, personal spending) categories. Tools like budgeting apps or spreadsheets can be invaluable here. Take the example of Michael, who realized he was spending an unsustainable amount on dining out, leading him to adjust his spending habits.

Step 4: Set Financial Goals

Define short-term (saving for a vacation, emergency fund) and long-term (retirement, down payment on a home) financial goals. This step helps prioritize your spending and savings. For someone like Sophia, setting a goal to save for a graduate degree shaped her budgeting strategy.

Step 5: Make Adjustments

Compare your income to your expenses. If you find your expenses exceed your income, look for areas to cut back. Conversely, if you have money left over, decide how to allocate it towards your goals. This is a critical step in ensuring your budget is realistic and achievable.

Step 6: Implement Your Budget

Put your budget into action. Track your spending and stay within the limits you've set. Use budgeting tools or apps to help you stay on track. Think of yourself as navigating your financial ship; regular checks and adjustments keep you moving in the right direction.

Step 7: Review and Adjust Regularly

Your financial situation and goals may change, so it's important to review your budget regularly and make necessary adjustments. Treat it as a living document that evolves with your life.

Example:

Step 1: Gather Your Financial Documents

Sarah, a marketing executive, begins her budgeting journey by collecting her bank statements, pay stubs, and bills. She wants to get a comprehensive view of her finances to make informed decisions.

Step 2: Calculate Your Total Income

After gathering her financial documents, Sarah calculates her total income. She includes her monthly salary of $4,000 and an additional $1,000 from freelance projects, totaling $5,000 per month.

Step 3: List Your Monthly Expenses

Sarah categorizes her expenses into fixed and variable categories. Her fixed expenses include rent at $1,200, utilities at $100, and a car payment of $300. Her variable expenses consist of groceries ($400), entertainment ($200), and shopping ($300).

Step 4: Set Financial Goals

Sarah sets her financial goals, aiming to build an emergency fund and save for a vacation. She decides to allocate $200 towards her emergency fund and $300 towards her vacation fund, totaling $500 in savings each month.

Step 5: Make Adjustments

After comparing her income to her expenses, Sarah realizes she needs to make adjustments to stay within her budget. She decides to reduce her shopping and dining out expenses by $50 each, bringing them down to $250 and $150, respectively.

Step 6: Implement Your Budget

Sarah puts her budget into action. She uses a budgeting app to track her spending and ensure she stays within her limits. By being mindful of her expenses, she manages to stick to her budget and even saves a little extra towards her goals.

Step 7: Review and Adjust Regularly

Sarah reviews her budget monthly to see if she's on track. She adjusts her budget as needed, such as increasing her savings goal after receiving a raise at work or reducing expenses if unexpected costs arise.

By following these steps, Sarah successfully creates a budget that aligns with her financial goals. Through careful planning and monitoring, she can achieve financial stability and work towards her dreams. Regular review and adjustments are key to maintaining a healthy budget and staying on track toward financial success.

Creating a budget is the first step in a journey toward financial mastery. It's about more than just numbers; it's a tool for achieving your dreams and securing your future. By following these steps, you can create a budget that reflects your values, supports your goals, and leads to a healthier financial life. Remember, every great journey begins with a single step. Let your budget be the step that moves you toward the financial stability and freedom you deserve.

1.2.3 Tips for Budgeting Success: Identifying and Cutting Unnecessary Expenses

In the quest for financial stability, budgeting emerges as a powerful tool, akin to a compass guiding you toward your financial goals. However, sticking to a budget can be challenging, especially when faced with the temptation to overspend on unnecessary items. To achieve budgeting success, it's crucial to identify and eliminate these unnecessary expenses. By doing so, you not only free up funds for more meaningful purposes but also cultivate a mindset of mindful spending. In this topic, we'll explore effective tips for identifying and cutting unnecessary expenses, paving the way for a more financially secure future.

Track Your Spending

The first step towards identifying unnecessary expenses is to track your spending. This could be done using budgeting apps or simply by keeping a record of your expenses. By doing so, you'll gain insight into where your money is going and identify areas where you can cut back.

Differentiate Between Needs and Wants

One of the key principles of budgeting success is understanding the difference between needs and wants. While needs are essential for survival, wants are desires that can often be postponed or eliminated. For example, while groceries are a need, dining out is a want. By prioritizing needs over wants, you can allocate more funds toward your financial goals.

Set Realistic Goals

Setting realistic financial goals is essential for successful budgeting. By having clear goals, you'll be motivated to cut back on unnecessary expenses. For instance, if your goal is to save for a vacation, you may decide to cut back on daily coffee purchases or dining out to free up funds for your trip.

Review Recurring Expenses

Recurring expenses, such as subscription services or memberships, can quickly add up. Take the time to review these expenses regularly and determine if they are worth the cost. For example, if you rarely use a gym membership, consider canceling it and finding alternative ways to stay active.

Practice Mindful Spending

Mindful spending involves being intentional about your purchases and avoiding impulse buys. Before making a purchase, ask yourself if it aligns with your financial goals and if it's something you truly need. For example, instead of buying a new outfit on a whim, you may decide to wait until it goes on sale or until you've saved up enough money.

Successfully managing your budget requires diligence and a willingness to make tough decisions. By identifying and cutting unnecessary expenses, you can free up funds for more meaningful purposes and work towards achieving your financial goals. Remember, every dollar saved is a step closer to financial freedom. By implementing these tips, you'll be on your way to budgeting success and a more secure financial future.

1.2.4 The Importance of Reviewing and Adjusting Your Budget Regularly

Imagine setting sail on a journey without a map or compass, hoping to reach your destination by sheer luck. Much like navigating uncharted waters, managing your finances without a budget review is a risky endeavor.

Regularly reviewing and adjusting your budget is the compass that keeps you on course toward your financial goals. It's not just about tracking expenses; it's about ensuring your financial plan remains relevant and effective in the ever-changing seas of life. In this topic, we'll explore the importance of reviewing and adjusting your budget regularly, and how it can lead to financial success and stability.

Adapting to Life Changes

Life is full of surprises, both good and bad. Whether it's a job change, a new addition to the family, or unexpected expenses, life events can impact your financial situation. By regularly reviewing and adjusting your budget, you can adapt to these changes and ensure your financial plan remains realistic and achievable.

Identifying and Eliminating Inefficiencies

Regular budget reviews can help you identify inefficiencies in your spending habits. Maybe you're spending more than you realize on dining out, or perhaps you're paying for services you no longer use. By identifying these inefficiencies, you can eliminate unnecessary expenses and free up funds for more important priorities.

Staying Motivated

Regularly reviewing your budget can help you stay motivated toward your financial goals. Seeing your progress and making adjustments as needed can keep you focused and committed to your plan. For example, if you're saving for a down payment on a house, reviewing your budget regularly can help you track your savings and stay motivated to reach your goal.

Preparing for the Unexpected

Life is unpredictable, and having a flexible budget can help you prepare for unexpected expenses. By regularly reviewing your budget and setting aside funds for emergencies, you can avoid financial stress when the unexpected occurs. For example, having an emergency fund can help you cover unexpected medical expenses or car repairs without derailing your financial plan.

In conclusion, regularly reviewing and adjusting your budget is essential for financial success. It allows you to adapt to life changes, identify inefficiencies, stay motivated, and prepare for the unexpected.

By making budgeting a regular part of your financial routine, you can ensure your financial plan remains effective and helps you achieve your long-term goals.

Remember, a budget is not a set-it-and-forget-it tool; it's a dynamic plan that evolves with your life.

1.3 Starting an Emergency Fund

1.3.1 What an emergency fund is and why it's important?

Imagine this: Your car suddenly breaks down, leaving you with a hefty repair bill, or an unexpected medical emergency arises, demanding immediate financial attention. Scenarios like these are not just hypotheticals; they are real-life situations that can occur at any moment. This is where the concept of an emergency fund not only enters the picture but becomes the hero of your financial narrative. An emergency fund is more than just a financial buzzword; it's a fundamental pillar of personal finance that acts as a buffer against life's unpredictable challenges.

1. What is an Emergency Fund?

An emergency fund, simply put, is a stash of money set aside to cover unexpected expenses or financial emergencies. These can range from sudden medical bills, job loss, urgent home repairs to any unforeseen financial needs that life throws your way. The key characteristic of this fund is its liquidity - the ability to access the money quickly and without penalty.

2. Why is an Emergency Fund Important?

- ❖ Financial Security: An emergency fund provides a financial safety net that can help you avoid debt. Without it, you might have to rely on credit cards or loans, leading to high interest and potential financial turmoil.
- ❖ Peace of Mind: Knowing you have a financial cushion can reduce stress and anxiety associated with unexpected expenses. It's not just about the money; it's also about the emotional and mental wellbeing that comes with being prepared.
- ❖ Empowering Financial Independence: With an emergency fund, you have the freedom to make decisions without being cornered by financial desperation. It empowers you to handle emergencies on your terms.

3. How Much Should You Save?

The size of your emergency fund will depend on various factors, including your lifestyle, monthly expenses, job stability, and whether you have dependents. A general rule of thumb is to have three to six months' worth of living expenses saved. However, this can vary based on individual circumstances.

4. Tips for Building Your Emergency Fund:

* Start Small: Even if it's just a few dollars each week, the important thing is to start. Over time, these small amounts will add up.
* Automate Your Savings: Set up an automatic transfer from your checking account to a savings account dedicated to your emergency fund. This makes the saving process effortless.
* Cut Back on Non-Essential Expenses: Review your spending habits and identify areas where you can cut back. Redirecting these funds to your emergency savings can accelerate your progress.

In life's grand tapestry, uncertainties are the only certainties. An emergency fund acts as a bulwark against these uncertainties, providing you with financial stability and peace of mind. Starting an emergency fund might seem daunting at first, but with consistent effort and smart financial decisions, it's an achievable goal. Remember, it's not about the amount you start with; it's about taking that first step towards securing your financial future. So, take that step today, and weave a safety net that holds you and your loved ones securely, come what may.

1.3.2 Guidelines for how much to save in an emergency fund

In the intricate dance of personal finance, establishing an emergency fund is akin to learning the first, crucial steps. However, once you understand the importance of this financial buffer, a pressing question arises: How much should you actually save in it? It's a question that looms large, bearing the weight of financial security and peace of mind. Striking the right balance in your emergency savings can mean the difference between financial buoyancy and sinking under unexpected expenses. This topic will serve as your compass in navigating these waters, offering clear guidelines and actionable steps to determine the ideal size of your emergency fund, ensuring you're well-prepared for life's unpredictable rhythms.

1. Understanding the Basics:

Before diving into numbers, let's revisit the purpose of an emergency fund. It's designed to cover essential expenses during unforeseen financial hardships like job loss, medical emergencies, or urgent home repairs. The essence of this fund is its liquidity—having access to funds when you most need them, without penalty.

2. How Much is Enough?

* Three to Six Months' Rule: The traditional advice is to save enough to cover three to six months of living expenses. This provides a substantial buffer to navigate through most short-term financial crises without falling into debt.
* Customizing Your Fund Size: The "one-size-fits-all" approach doesn't apply to emergency funds. Consider factors like job stability, income streams, monthly expenses, and family obligations. For example, freelancers or those with fluctuating incomes might aim for a larger buffer, whereas individuals with stable jobs and fewer dependents could adjust their target accordingly.

3. Calculating Your Target Emergency Fund Size:

- ❖ List Your Monthly Expenses: Start with fixed expenses (rent/mortgage, utilities, insurance) and variable expenses (groceries, fuel, personal spending). Don't forget about occasional expenses that can be prorated monthly (annual subscriptions, maintenance costs).
- ❖ Adjust for Realistic Scenarios: Consider potential cost reductions during a financial crisis (e.g., cutting back on discretionary spending). This adjusted monthly cost provides a more accurate target for your emergency fund.

4. Steps to Building Your Emergency Fund:

- ❖ Set a Monthly Saving Goal: Based on your calculated target, determine a realistic monthly saving amount. Even small contributions can build over time.
- ❖ Increase Your Income: Look for opportunities to boost your income through side gigs, overtime, or selling unused items. This extra income can accelerate your emergency fund growth.
- ❖ Use Windfalls Wisely: Tax refunds, bonuses, and other financial windfalls should be partially allocated to your emergency fund.

Your emergency fund is your financial lifeline, offering a buffer against life's uncertainties. While the journey to amassing three to six months' worth of expenses may seem daunting, remember that each step you take is a stride towards financial resilience. By customizing your savings target to your personal circumstances and adopting a disciplined approach to building your fund, you're not just saving money—you're investing in your peace of mind and financial security. Start today, and navigate your way to a more secure financial future, prepared for whatever storms may come your way.

1.3.3 Tips for building an emergency fund, such as automating savings and starting small.

Picture your financial landscape as a bustling cityscape, where your emergency fund is a crucial bridge connecting you safely over unforeseen challenges. The journey to constructing this bridge can seem daunting, especially when starting from the ground up. However, the path to financial security doesn't require grand gestures but rather, small, consistent steps in the right direction. In this topic, we'll explore actionable strategies to build and strengthen your emergency fund, turning a daunting task into an achievable goal. From automating your savings to starting with what you might consider insignificant amounts, we're here to guide you through making your emergency fund a pillar of your financial resilience.

1. The Power of Starting Small:

- ❖ The "Spare Change" Approach: Begin by saving loose change or rounding up your purchases to the nearest dollar, depositing the difference into your emergency fund. Over time, these small amounts can accumulate into a substantial sum.
- ❖ Set Small, Achievable Goals: Aim to save a modest amount weekly or monthly. Achieving these small milestones can boost your confidence and encourage you to continue saving.

2. Automating Your Savings:

- ❖ Direct Deposit from Paycheck: Arrange for a portion of your paycheck to be directly deposited into a separate savings account designated for emergencies. This "out of sight, out of mind" strategy prevents the temptation to spend what you've earmarked for saving.
- ❖ Scheduled Transfers: Utilize your bank's online banking platform to set up automatic transfers from your checking to your savings account, aligning with your pay schedule.

3. Cutting Costs to Boost Your Emergency Fund:

* Review and Reduce Non-Essential Spending: Identify areas where you can cut back, such as dining out, subscription services, or discretionary shopping. Redirect these savings to your emergency fund.
* Embrace Frugality: Adopt cost-saving measures like using coupons, shopping sales, and considering second-hand options when possible.

4. Finding Additional Income Sources:

* Monetize Your Skills or Hobbies: Consider freelancing, tutoring, or selling handmade goods to generate extra income.
* Sell Unneeded Items: Declutter your home and sell items you no longer use or need. This not only frees up space but also boosts your emergency savings.

5. Keeping Your Emergency Fund Accessible but Separate:

* Choose the Right Savings Vehicle: Your emergency fund should be easily accessible but kept in a separate account from your daily checking. High-yield savings accounts are a great option, offering higher interest rates while ensuring liquidity.

Building an emergency fund is a foundational step towards financial stability, acting as a safeguard against life's unexpected turns. Starting small, automating your savings, cutting unnecessary costs, finding additional sources of income, and wisely choosing where to keep your fund are all manageable strategies to grow your emergency savings. Remember, the journey to a robust emergency fund begins with a single step. By applying these tips, you'll not only pave the way to financial security but also cultivate habits that support sustained financial health. Start building your financial buffer today, and watch as your emergency fund transforms from a fledgling account into a cornerstone of your financial resilience.

52 Weeks saving plan:

Creating a 52-week savings plan aimed at gradually increasing savings over time can be an effective strategy to reach a substantial goal by the end of the year. To achieve a 100% savings goal over 52 weeks, the plan can start with a small, manageable amount and incrementally increase, or it can vary based on expected fluctuations in one's ability to save. For simplicity and motivation, let's start with a base model where you save a bit more each week in a linear progression.

This model assumes that "100%" represents a monetary goal you've set for the year. For simplicity, let's say your goal is to save $1,378 by the end of the year because this amount aligns well with a straightforward incremental plan. Adjust the starting point and increments as necessary to fit your specific financial target.

52-Week Savings Plan:

- Week 1: Save $1.00 - Total: $1.00
- Week 2: Save $2.00 - Total: $3.00
- Week 3: Save $3.00 - Total: $6.00
- Week 4: Save $4.00 - Total: $10.00
- Week 5: Save $5.00 - Total: $15.00
- Week 6: Save $6.00 - Total: $21.00
- Week 7: Save $7.00 - Total: $28.00
- Week 8: Save $8.00 - Total: $36.00
- Week 9: Save $9.00 - Total: $45.00
- Week 10: Save $10.00 - Total: $55.00
- Week 11 to Week 52: Continue increasing your savings by $1 more than the previous week.

By following this plan, in the final week (Week 52), you will save $52.00, and your total savings for the year will be $1,378.

This incremental increase serves dual purposes: it eases you into saving by starting with a very manageable amount and gradually adjusts your budget to accommodate higher savings rates. The beauty of this approach is its simplicity and adaptability; you can adjust the increment or start amount to align with your specific savings goal.

For example, if your goal is higher, you could start Week 1 by saving $2.00 and then increase by $2.00 every week thereafter, or adjust the plan according to your income and savings goals. The key to success is consistency and adaptability to your financial situation.

Your emergency fund is your financial lifeline, offering a buffer against life's uncertainties. While the journey to amassing three to six months' worth of expenses may seem daunting, remember that each step you take is a stride towards financial resilience. By customizing your savings target to your personal circumstances and adopting a disciplined approach to building your fund, you're not just saving money—you're investing in your peace of mind and financial security. Start today, and navigate your way to a more secure financial future, prepared for whatever storms may come your way.

1.4 Understanding Credit Scores

1.4.1 What a credit score is and how it is calculated.

Navigating the financial landscape without understanding the calculation of your credit score is like setting sail without a compass. Your credit score, a crucial determinant of your financial health, can either open up a realm of possibilities or serve as a stumbling block to achieving your dreams. Through the contrasting financial journeys of two individuals, Emma and Liam, this topic demystifies the complex algorithm behind credit score calculation, offering you the keys to unlocking a brighter financial future.

Imagine standing at a crossroad where one path leads to a lush oasis of financial opportunities, while the other descends into a desert of high-interest rates and declined loan applications. Your credit score—the invisible guide—determines your direction. But what wizardry calculates this pivotal number? Meet Emma and Liam, two friends with similar incomes and lifestyles, yet their credit scores tell a dramatically different story. As we unveil the secrets behind these scores, you'll discover how small financial behaviors can lead to significant impacts on your creditworthiness.

The Anatomy of Your Credit Score

- **Payment History (35%)**: This is like your report card showing how punctually you've paid your bills. Late payments are red flags, akin to Taylor's delayed book returns.
- **Credit Utilization (30%)**: This measures how much of your available credit you're using. It's the difference between someone who uses a small portion of their borrowing limit versus someone maxing out their credit cards. Responsible use here signals to lenders that you're not overly dependent on credit.

❖ **Length of Credit History (15%)**: The longer your history of managing credit, the better. It's the difference between a seasoned employee and a new hire; experience counts.

❖ **New Credit (10%)**: This looks at how many new accounts you've opened recently. Opening many new accounts in a short period can be seen as financial desperation, akin to suddenly borrowing money from several friends.

❖ **Credit Mix (10%)**: Having a variety of credit types (e.g., mortgage, car loan, credit cards) shows you can handle different types of debt responsibly.

Understanding and nurturing your credit score is akin to maintaining a key to the financial kingdom. It can swing doors wide open to better loan rates, higher borrowing limits, and even affect your job prospects. Start by regularly checking your credit report for inaccuracies, paying bills on time, and managing your debts wisely. Remember, improving your credit score is a journey, not a sprint. By treating your credit with the respect it deserves, you're not just enhancing numbers on a page; you're paving the way for a more secure financial future. Let your credit score reflect not just your financial history, but your financial acumen.

In the vast ocean of fiscal responsibilities, let it be your guiding lighthouse, ensuring you safely navigate towards your dreams.

Example: Emma vs. Liam – A Comparative Analysis

- ❖ **Payment History**: Emma has a pristine payment history, never missing a payment deadline. In contrast, Liam has a history of late payments and even a few missed payments. These discrepancies significantly impact their credit scores, as payment history accounts for 35% of the score.
- ❖ **Credit Utilization**: Emma maintains a low credit utilization ratio, typically using less than 30% of her available credit. Liam, however, frequently maxes out his credit cards, leading to a high utilization ratio. This factor accounts for 30% of the credit score calculation.
- ❖ **Length of Credit History**: Emma has a long credit history, having maintained her first credit account for over a decade. Liam, on the other hand, has a relatively short credit history, having opened his first credit account only a few years ago. The length of credit history comprises 15% of the credit score.

* **New Credit**: Emma is cautious about opening new credit accounts, as each application can result in a hard inquiry, which temporarily lowers the credit score. Liam, however, frequently applies for new credit cards, leading to multiple hard inquiries and a negative impact on his score. This factor contributes to 10% of the credit score.

* **Credit Mix**: Emma has a diverse credit portfolio, including a mortgage, a car loan, and several credit cards. Liam, on the other hand, relies heavily on credit cards and has limited experience with other types of credit. Credit mix makes up 10% of the credit score calculation.

Emma and Liam's stories serve as cautionary tales, illustrating the impact of financial decisions on credit scores. By paying bills on time, maintaining low credit card balances, keeping credit accounts open, applying for credit sparingly, and diversifying credit types, you can improve your credit score and secure a brighter financial future. Your credit score is not set in stone; it's a dynamic reflection of your financial behavior. By understanding the factors that influence it, you can take control of your financial destiny and steer towards a path of financial stability and prosperity.

1.4.2 The importance of a good credit score in financial health.

In the intricate tapestry of personal finance, few threads are as crucial as your credit score. This unassuming number wields immense power, influencing not just your ability to borrow money but also the terms on which you can borrow. Whether you're applying for a mortgage, a car loan, or even a job, your credit score can be the deciding factor. Join us as we explore the profound impact of a good credit score on your financial health and unravel the key to unlocking a brighter financial future.

Imagine you're standing at the threshold of your dream home, keys in hand, ready to embark on a new chapter of your life. Now, imagine being turned away because of a three-digit number. This scenario may seem far-fetched, but for many individuals with poor credit scores, it's a stark reality. Your credit score is more than just a number; it's a reflection of your financial responsibility and trustworthiness in the eyes of lenders.

- ❖ **Access to Credit**: A good credit score opens doors to a world of credit opportunities. Lenders are more likely to approve your applications for loans and credit cards, and you'll often qualify for lower interest rates and better terms. This means you can borrow money when you need it without breaking the bank.
- ❖ **Lower Interest Rates**: One of the most significant benefits of a good credit score is the ability to secure loans and credit cards at lower interest rates. For example, let's consider two individuals, Sarah and Mike, both applying for a $20,000 car loan. Sarah has a credit score of 750, while Mike's score is 600. Sarah qualifies for a 5% interest rate, while Mike is offered a rate of 10%. Over the life of the loan, Sarah would pay significantly less in interest, saving her thousands of dollars.

❖ **Better Insurance Rates**: Believe it or not, your credit score can also affect your insurance premiums. Many insurance companies use credit scores as a factor in determining premiums for auto and homeowners insurance. A good credit score can lead to lower insurance rates, saving you money each month.

❖ **Employment Opportunities**: Some employers check credit scores as part of the hiring process, especially for positions that involve financial responsibility. A good credit score can improve your chances of landing a job, as it demonstrates your ability to manage finances responsibly.

Your credit score is not just a number; it's a key that can unlock a world of financial opportunities. By maintaining a good credit score, you can enjoy lower interest rates, better loan terms, and even improved job prospects. Start by regularly checking your credit report for errors, paying bills on time, and keeping your credit card balances low. By taking control of your credit score, you're taking control of your financial future.

1.4.3 Tips for improving or maintaining a good credit score, such as paying bills on time and keeping credit card balances low.

In the vast landscape of personal finance, your credit score is the compass guiding your financial journey. A good credit score opens doors to favorable loan terms, lower interest rates, and even employment opportunities. But maintaining or improving this critical number requires a strategic approach. Join us as we uncover the tried-and-true tips for enhancing and preserving your credit score, empowering you to navigate the financial terrain with confidence and savvy.

Picture this: You're eyeing that dream car or perhaps a new home, and your credit score stands between you and your goal. It's not just a number; it's the key to unlocking your financial aspirations. By implementing simple yet powerful strategies, you can not only boost your credit score but also sustain it at an optimal level. Let's dive into the strategies that can elevate your credit score game and set you on the path to financial success.

- ❖ **Pay Bills on Time**: Timely payment of bills is crucial for maintaining a good credit score. Set up automatic payments or reminders to ensure you never miss a due date. Even a single missed payment can have a significant impact on your score.

- ❖ **Keep Credit Card Balances Low**: Aim to keep your credit card balances below 30% of your credit limit. High credit card balances can indicate financial stress and may lower your credit score. Paying off balances in full each month is ideal, but if that's not possible, strive to keep balances as low as possible.

- ❖ **Monitor Your Credit Report Regularly**: Stay vigilant by monitoring your credit report regularly for errors or unauthorized accounts. You're entitled to a free credit report from each of the three major credit bureaus (Equifax, Experian, and TransUnion) every 12 months.

- ❖ **Limit New Credit Applications**: Each time you apply for new credit, a hard inquiry is placed on your credit report, which can lower your score. Limiting the number of new credit applications can help maintain your score.

- ❖ **Diversify Your Credit Mix**: Having a mix of credit types, such as credit cards, installment loans, and a mortgage, can positively impact your credit score. This demonstrates to lenders that you can manage different types of credit responsibly.

Your credit score is a reflection of your financial habits and decisions. By following these simple yet effective tips, you can not only improve your credit score but also maintain it at a level that opens doors to financial opportunities. Remember, building a strong credit score is a journey, not a destination. Stay committed to smart financial habits, and your credit score will pave the way to a brighter financial future.

In conclusion, mastering the art of credit scores is not just about understanding the numbers; it's about adopting smart financial habits that can lead to a lifetime of financial success. By taking control of your credit score and implementing these strategies, you can pave the way to a brighter financial future and unlock a world of opportunities.

1.5 Debt Management

1.5.1 What is debt? and Different types of debt.

Debt, a ubiquitous term in the realm of finance, is both a lifeline and a potential pitfall for individuals and businesses alike. It's the financial force that enables dreams—a home, a college education, a thriving business—but if mishandled, it can quickly spiral into a nightmare of insurmountable proportions. Understanding debt is not just about knowing how much you owe; it's about grasping the nuances of its types, its impact, and its potential to shape your financial future.

In this topic, we embark on a journey to unravel the complexities of debt. We'll delve into the various forms it takes, from everyday credit card debt to the substantial commitments of mortgage loans.

Through real-life examples and practical insights, we aim to demystify debt, empowering you to navigate the borrowing landscape with confidence and clarity.

❖ **Consumer Debt:** Consumer debt, often a gateway to financial independence, encompasses the loans and balances we incur in our daily lives. Imagine Sarah, a recent college graduate, who, eager to furnish her new apartment, swipes her credit card without much thought. Before she knows it, she's accumulated a significant balance, complete with high-interest charges. This scenario illustrates the allure and danger of consumer debt—it's easy to access but can quickly become overwhelming if not managed wisely.

❖ **Mortgage Debt:** For many, owning a home is the pinnacle of the American Dream. Yet, achieving this dream often requires taking on mortgage debt. Consider Alex and Maria, a young couple looking to buy their first home. They secure a mortgage, leveraging the property as collateral. While this debt comes with the benefit of homeownership, it also carries the weight of long-term financial commitment.

- ❖ **Student Loans:** Education is often hailed as the key to a brighter future. However, for many students, this pursuit comes with a hefty price tag. Take David, a graduate student pursuing a degree in engineering. To fund his education, he takes out student loans, hoping that his investment will pay off in the form of higher earning potential. While student loans offer a path to education, they also saddle graduates with significant debt burdens.

- ❖ **Business Debt**: Entrepreneurs often rely on debt to fuel the growth and expansion of their businesses. Consider Rachel, who starts a small bakery and takes out a business loan to purchase equipment and hire staff. While this debt allows her business to thrive, it also adds a layer of financial complexity and risk.

Debt is a multifaceted financial tool that can pave the way for progress or lead to financial hardship. By understanding its various forms and implications, you can make informed borrowing decisions. Remember, debt is not inherently good or bad; it's how you manage it that determines its impact on your financial well-being. So, as you navigate the world of finance, may you wield the power of debt wisely, shaping a future that is both prosperous and sustainable.

1.5.2 Conquering Debt: Strategies for Effective Management and Reduction

Debt, like a shadow, follows many of us throughout our lives, casting a looming presence over our financial freedom. Yet, despite its pervasive nature, debt is not insurmountable. With the right strategies, you can take control of your financial future and pave the way to a debt-free life. In this topic, we explore two powerful methods for managing and reducing debt—the debt snowball and debt avalanche. By understanding these strategies and how to implement them, you can embark on a journey towards financial freedom.

- ❖ **Debt Snowball Method**: The debt snowball method is a debt reduction strategy popularized by personal finance guru Dave Ramsey. It involves paying off your debts from smallest to largest, regardless of interest rate, while making minimum payments on all other debts. This approach focuses on building momentum and motivation by quickly eliminating smaller debts.

For example, consider Emma, who has three credit cards with balances of $500, $1,000, and $2,000. Using the debt snowball method, she would first pay off the $500 balance, then the $1,000 balance, and finally the $2,000 balance. As each debt is paid off, she rolls the amount she was paying on that debt into the next debt, creating a snowball effect that accelerates her progress.

- ❖ **Debt Avalanche Method**: The debt avalanche method, in contrast, prioritizes debts based on interest rate, rather than balance. With this approach, you focus on paying off the debt with the highest interest rate first, while continuing to make minimum payments on all other debts. Once the highest-interest debt is paid off, you move on to the debt with the next highest interest rate, and so on. While the debt avalanche method may not provide the immediate gratification of the debt snowball, it can save you money on interest payments in the long run.

For example, Sarah has two loans—a credit card balance with an interest rate of 20% and a personal loan with an interest rate of 10%. Using the debt avalanche method, she would first pay off the credit card balance, as it has the higher interest rate, before tackling the personal loan.

Managing and reducing debt is a journey that requires commitment and discipline. By utilizing strategies such as the debt snowball or debt avalanche method, you can take control of your finances and work towards a debt-free future. Whether you choose to focus on small victories with the debt snowball method or prioritize interest savings with the debt avalanche method, the key is to stay focused and keep moving forward. With determination and perseverance, you can conquer your debt and achieve financial freedom.

1.5.3 Mastering Debt: The Art of Consolidation and Refinancing

Debt can often feel like a heavy burden, weighing down your financial freedom and limiting your options. However, there are strategies available that can help you manage your debt more effectively, such as debt consolidation and refinancing. These methods can simplify your finances, potentially reduce your interest rates, and make your debt more manageable. In this topic, we'll dive deeper into the world of debt consolidation and refinancing, exploring their benefits, drawbacks, and how they can help you on your journey to financial freedom.

Debt Consolidation:

Debt consolidation involves combining multiple debts into a single loan, typically with a lower interest rate and a more manageable repayment schedule. This can be especially helpful if you have high-interest debts, such as credit card balances. By consolidating your debts, you can streamline your payments and potentially save money on interest. For example, Sarah has three credit cards with varying balances and interest rates. By consolidating her credit card debt into a single loan, she can simplify her payments and potentially lower her overall interest costs. However, it's important to carefully consider the terms and fees associated with debt consolidation, as well as the impact it may have on your credit score.

Pros:

- ❖ Simplified Repayment: One of the main benefits of debt consolidation is that it combines multiple debts into a single loan, making it easier to manage your payments. Instead of juggling multiple due dates and payment amounts, you only have to worry about one monthly payment.
- ❖ Potentially Lower Interest Rates: By consolidating your debts into a single loan, you may be able to secure a lower interest rate than what you were

paying on your individual debts. This can save you money on interest over time and help you pay off your debt faster.

❖ Fixed Repayment Terms: Debt consolidation loans often come with fixed repayment terms, which means you'll know exactly how long it will take to pay off your debt. This can help you budget and plan for your financial future more effectively.

❖ Improved Credit Score: If you're able to make your debt consolidation loan payments on time and in full, it can have a positive impact on your credit score. Having a single, manageable payment can make it easier to stay on top of your payments and improve your creditworthiness.

Cons:

❖ Potential Fees: Some debt consolidation loans come with fees, such as origination fees or prepayment penalties. These fees can add to the overall cost of the loan and reduce the potential savings from consolidating your debt.

❖ Risk of Accumulating More Debt: Consolidating your debts can free up credit on your other accounts, such as credit cards. This can be tempting and lead to further debt accumulation if you're not careful about managing your finances.

- ❖ Longer Repayment Terms: While debt consolidation can lower your monthly payments, it can also extend the repayment term of your debt. This means you may end up paying more in interest over the life of the loan compared to if you had paid off your debts individually.

- ❖ Impact on Credit Score: Applying for a new loan can temporarily lower your credit score, as it can result in a hard inquiry on your credit report. Additionally, if you close any of your old accounts after consolidating your debt, it can affect your credit utilization ratio, which is a factor in your credit score.

Overall, debt consolidation can be a helpful tool for managing debt, but it's important to carefully consider the pros and cons and assess your financial situation before deciding if it's the right choice for you.

Refinancing:

Refinancing involves replacing an existing loan with a new loan, typically with more favorable terms. This can include obtaining a lower interest rate, extending the repayment period, or changing from a variable to a fixed interest rate. For example, John has a mortgage with a high-interest rate. By refinancing his mortgage, he can lower his monthly payments and potentially save thousands of dollars over the life of the loan. However, refinancing often involves closing costs and other fees, so it's important to carefully weigh the potential savings against the upfront costs.

Pros:

- ❖ Lower Interest Rates: One of the primary reasons people refinance is to secure a lower interest rate on their loan. A lower interest rate can save you money on interest payments over the life of the loan, resulting in lower monthly payments.
- ❖ Reduced Monthly Payments: Refinancing can also lead to reduced monthly payments, either by extending the loan term or obtaining a lower interest rate. This can free up cash flow for other expenses or savings goals.
- ❖ Change in Loan Term: Refinancing allows you to change the term of your loan. For example, you can

switch from a 30-year mortgage to a 15-year mortgage, which can help you pay off your loan faster and save on interest.

* Cash-Out Option: Some refinancing options allow you to borrow more than the remaining balance on your current loan and receive the difference in cash. This can be useful for home improvements, debt consolidation, or other financial needs.

Cons:

* Closing Costs: Refinancing typically involves closing costs, which can include application fees, appraisal fees, and other fees. These costs can add up and offset the savings you may gain from refinancing.
* Extended Loan Term: While refinancing can reduce your monthly payments, it can also extend the term of your loan. This means you may end up paying more in interest over the life of the loan compared to your original loan.
* Impact on Credit Score: Applying for a refinance requires a hard inquiry on your credit report, which can temporarily lower your credit score. Additionally, if you close your old loan after refinancing, it can affect your credit mix and

average account age, which are factors in your credit score.

- ❖ Risk of Foreclosure: If you refinance a mortgage and are unable to keep up with the new payments, you could be at risk of foreclosure. It's important to carefully consider your ability to afford the new loan terms before refinancing.

Overall, refinancing can be a beneficial financial move if it helps you save money on interest, lower your monthly payments, or achieve other financial goals. However, it's important to weigh the pros and cons and carefully consider your financial situation before refinancing.

Debt consolidation and refinancing can be powerful tools for managing and reducing debt, but they're not without their drawbacks. Before pursuing either strategy, it's important to carefully evaluate your financial situation and goals. Consider the potential benefits and drawbacks, and consult with a financial advisor if needed. With careful planning and consideration, you can use these strategies to take control of your debt and work towards a more secure financial future.

In conclusion, effective debt management is essential for achieving financial stability and freedom. Whether you choose to consolidate your debts, refinance existing loans, or use other strategies, the key is to have a clear plan and stay disciplined in your approach. By understanding the pros and cons of different debt management strategies and tailoring them to your financial goals, you can take control of your debt and work towards a brighter financial future. Remember, the journey to debt-free living may not be easy, but with determination and smart financial choices, you can achieve your goals and build a solid foundation for long-term financial health.

1.6 Investing Basics

1.6.1 Understanding the Concept of Investing and Its Potential Benefits

Investing is a powerful financial tool that can help individuals grow their wealth over time. It involves committing money to an asset or endeavor with the expectation of generating a profit or an increase in value. While investing comes with risks, understanding the basics and potential benefits can help individuals make informed decisions to secure their financial future.

1. **What is Investing?**

    - Investing is the act of allocating resources, usually money, with the expectation of generating an income or profit.
    - Common types of investments include stocks, bonds, real estate, and mutual funds.

2. **Benefits of Investing:**

    - **Wealth Growth:** Investing allows individuals to grow their wealth over time through the power of compounding returns. By reinvesting earnings, investments can generate additional income.
    - **Financial Security:** Investing can provide a source of passive income, which can help individuals achieve financial security and independence.
    - **Beat Inflation:** Investing in assets that outpace inflation can help preserve the purchasing power of money over time.
    - **Achieve Financial Goals:** Whether it's buying a home, funding education, or retiring comfortably, investing can help individuals achieve their financial goals.

3. **Key Considerations for Investing:**
   - ➤ **Risk Tolerance:** Understanding your risk tolerance is crucial, as different investments come with varying levels of risk.
   - ➤ **Diversification:** Spreading investments across different asset classes can help reduce risk and protect against market volatility.
   - ➤ **Time Horizon:** The length of time you plan to hold an investment can impact your investment strategy.
4. **Examples of Investing:**
   - ➤ **Stock Market:** Investing in individual stocks or exchange-traded funds (ETFs) can provide exposure to the potential growth of companies.
   - ➤ **Real Estate:** Investing in real estate properties can generate rental income and property appreciation over time.
   - ➤ **Retirement Accounts:** Contributing to retirement accounts such as 401(k)s or IRAs can help individuals save for retirement with potential tax benefits.

In conclusion, investing is a powerful tool that can help individuals achieve their financial goals and secure their future. By understanding the concept of investing, its potential benefits, and key considerations, individuals can make informed decisions to build wealth over time. It's important to remember that investing involves risks, and seeking professional advice can help navigate the complexities of the investment landscape.

Example:

Let's consider two individuals, Alex and Sam, both 25 years old, who each have $5,000 to invest. Alex decides to start investing in the stock market, while Sam chooses not to invest and keeps his money in a savings account.

1. **Setting Investment Goals:**
   - Alex sets a goal to save for retirement and aims to retire at 65 with a comfortable nest egg. He plans to invest for the long term, around 40 years.
   - Sam does not have a specific investment goal and is more focused on saving for short-term needs and emergencies.
2. **Investment Strategy:**
   - Alex decides to invest his $5,000 in a diversified portfolio of stocks and bonds. He plans to contribute an additional $200 per month to his investment portfolio.

   - Sam keeps his $5,000 in a savings account with an interest rate of 0.5% per year, with no additional contributions.

3. **Understanding Risk Tolerance:**
   - Alex has a moderate risk tolerance and is willing to accept some fluctuations in the value of his investments in exchange for potentially higher returns.
   - Sam has a low risk tolerance and prefers the stability and security of a savings account, even though it offers lower returns.
4. **Investment Performance Over Time:**
   - After 10 years:
     - Alex's investments have grown to approximately $40,000, assuming an average annual return of 7%.
     - Sam's savings account balance has grown to approximately $6,500, assuming the same interest rate of 0.5% per year.
   - After 30 years:
     - Alex's investments have grown to approximately $340,000, assuming the same 7% average annual return.
     - Sam's savings account balance has grown to approximately $10,500, still with the same interest rate.

- ➢ After 40 years:
  - ▪ Alex's investments have grown to approximately $890,000, assuming the same 7% average annual return.
  - ▪ Sam's savings account balance has grown to approximately $14,500.

5. **Comparison:**
   - ➢ Alex's decision to invest has significantly outperformed Sam's decision not to invest.
   - ➢ By investing in a diversified portfolio, Alex has been able to take advantage of the power of compounding returns over time, resulting in a much larger investment portfolio compared to Sam's savings account.

6. **Conclusion:**
   - ➢ This example illustrates the importance of investing early and regularly to achieve long-term financial goals.
   - ➢ While investing comes with risk, it also offers the potential for higher returns compared to traditional savings accounts.
   - ➢ By understanding your investment goals, risk tolerance, and starting early, you can build a solid foundation for financial security and growth over time.

1.6.2 Exploring Investment Options: Stocks, Bonds, and Mutual Funds

Investing is a crucial aspect of financial planning, but the variety of investment options can be overwhelming. Understanding the basics of different investment options, such as stocks, bonds, and mutual funds, can help individuals make informed decisions to build wealth and achieve financial goals.

1. **Stocks:**
   - Stocks represent ownership in a company and are bought and sold on stock exchanges.
   - Investing in stocks can offer the potential for high returns but comes with higher risk due to market volatility.
   - Examples: Buying shares of Apple (AAPL) or Google (GOOGL) gives you ownership in these companies.
2. **Bonds:**
   - Bonds are debt securities issued by governments or corporations to raise capital.
   - Investing in bonds involves lending money to the issuer in exchange for periodic interest payments and the return of the bond's face value at maturity.
   - Bonds are generally considered safer than stocks but offer lower returns.

> Examples: Investing in U.S. Treasury bonds or corporate bonds.

3. **Mutual Funds:**

   > Mutual funds pool money from multiple investors to invest in a diversified portfolio of stocks, bonds, or other securities.

   > Mutual funds are managed by professional fund managers, who make investment decisions on behalf of investors.

   > Mutual funds offer diversification and are suitable for investors looking for a hands-off approach to investing.

   > Examples: Investing in a mutual fund that tracks the S&P 500 index provides exposure to a diversified portfolio of large-cap U.S. stocks.

4. **Key Considerations:**

   > Risk Tolerance: Different investment options come with varying levels of risk, and it's important to align your investments with your risk tolerance.

   > Investment Goals: Your investment goals, such as capital preservation, income generation, or wealth accumulation, should guide your choice of investment options.

   > Diversification: Building a diversified investment portfolio can help reduce risk and maximize returns.

In conclusion, understanding the different investment options, such as stocks, bonds, and mutual funds, is essential for building a successful investment portfolio. Each option has its own risk and return characteristics, and choosing the right mix of investments depends on your individual financial goals and risk tolerance. By diversifying your investments and staying informed, you can work towards achieving financial security and growth.

1.6.3 The Power of Diversification: Why It Matters in Your Investment Portfolio

Building a strong investment portfolio is like constructing a sturdy house. Just as a house needs a solid foundation, your portfolio needs diversification. Diversification is not just a buzzword; it's a crucial strategy that can help protect your investments from market volatility and enhance long-term returns. Let's explore why diversification is key to a successful investment strategy.

1. **What is Diversification?**
   - Diversification is the practice of spreading your investments across different asset classes, industries, and geographic regions.
   - The goal of diversification is to reduce risk by ensuring that a single event, such as a market downturn in one sector, doesn't have a catastrophic impact on your entire portfolio.

2. **Benefits of Diversification:**
   - **Risk Reduction:** Diversifying your investments can help mitigate the impact of market fluctuations on your portfolio.
   - **Enhanced Returns:** By spreading your investments across different assets, you increase the likelihood of capturing gains from various sources.
   - **Stability:** Diversification can provide a more stable investment experience, as losses in one asset class may be offset by gains in another.

3. **How to Diversify Your Portfolio:**
   - **Asset Classes:** Invest in a mix of stocks, bonds, and cash equivalents to spread risk.
   - **Industry Sectors:** Allocate investments across different industries to avoid concentration risk.
   - **Geographic Regions:** Consider investing in both domestic and international markets to diversify geopolitical risk.

➤ **Diversified Funds:** Mutual funds and exchange-traded funds (ETFs) offer instant diversification by pooling investments in a range of assets.

4. **Example of Diversification:**

➤ Suppose you invest all your money in the technology sector. If the tech industry experiences a downturn, your portfolio would suffer significant losses. However, if you diversified your investments across sectors like healthcare, consumer goods, and energy, a downturn in one sector would have a lesser impact on your overall portfolio.

In conclusion, diversification is a fundamental principle of investing that can help manage risk and enhance returns. By spreading your investments across different asset classes, industries, and regions, you can build a resilient portfolio that can weather market volatility and help you achieve your financial goals. Remember, the key to successful diversification is balance and thoughtful asset allocation based on your risk tolerance and investment objectives.

1.6.4 Tips for Setting Goals and Understanding Risk
Tolerance

Introduction: Embarking on your investment journey can
be both exciting and daunting. Setting clear investment
goals and understanding your risk tolerance are essential
first steps. Whether you're saving for retirement, a down
payment on a house, or simply looking to grow your
wealth, the following tips will help you get started on the
right foot.

1. **Set Clear Investment Goals:**
    - **Short-Term vs. Long-Term:** Determine if your
      goals are short-term (1-5 years) or long-term (10+
      years). Short-term goals may include saving for a
      vacation or a new car, while long-term goals could
      be saving for retirement or your child's education.
    - **Specific and Measurable:** Make your goals
      specific and measurable. Instead of saying "I want
      to save money," say "I want to save $10,000 for a
      down payment on a house in five years."
    - **Realistic and Achievable:** Set goals that are
      realistic and achievable based on your current
      financial situation and income.

2. **Understand Your Risk Tolerance:**
   - ➢ **Risk vs. Reward:** Understand that investing involves risk, and higher potential returns typically come with higher risk. Assess your comfort level with risk and volatility.
   - ➢ **Conservative vs. Aggressive:** Determine if you are more conservative (preferring lower-risk investments with potentially lower returns) or aggressive (willing to take on more risk for potentially higher returns).
   - ➢ **Diversification:** Consider diversifying your portfolio to manage risk. Diversification involves investing in a mix of different asset classes, such as stocks, bonds, and cash equivalents.

3. **Start Investing Early and Consistently:**
   - ➢ **Power of Compounding:** The earlier you start investing, the more time your money has to grow due to the power of compounding returns.
   - ➢ **Consistent Contributions:** Set up automatic contributions to your investment accounts to ensure consistent investing, regardless of market fluctuations.

4. **Educate Yourself and Seek Professional Advice:**
   - ➢ **Research and Learn:** Take the time to educate yourself about different investment options, strategies, and market trends.

> **Consult a Financial Advisor:** Consider seeking advice from a financial advisor to help you create a personalized investment plan based on your goals and risk tolerance.

Getting started with investing is an important step towards achieving your financial goals. By setting clear investment goals, understanding your risk tolerance, starting early, and educating yourself, you can build a solid foundation for a successful investment journey. Remember, investing is a long-term commitment, so stay focused on your goals and be prepared to adjust your investment strategy as needed.

In conclusion, investing is a powerful financial tool that, when approached with a clear strategy and understanding, can help individuals achieve their financial goals and secure their future. Diversification is key to building a resilient investment portfolio, as it helps mitigate risk and maximize returns by spreading investments across different asset classes, industries, and regions.

Setting clear investment goals, understanding risk tolerance, and starting early are fundamental steps to getting started with investing. By setting specific and measurable goals, assessing risk tolerance, and starting with small, consistent contributions, individuals can lay a strong foundation for a successful investment journey.

It's important to educate yourself about different investment options and seek professional advice to create a personalized investment plan that aligns with your goals and risk tolerance. Remember, investing is a long-term commitment, so stay focused on your goals and be prepared to adjust your investment strategy as needed to achieve financial security and growth.

1.7 **Saving for Retirement**

1.7.1 Start Saving for Retirement Early: Why It Matters More Than You Think

Are you one of those who often find themselves contemplating retirement as a far-off event that can be dealt with later? Well, it's time to pause and reconsider. Retirement may seem distant, but the sooner you start saving, the better off you'll be in the long run. In this topic, we'll delve into why saving for retirement early is crucial, exploring its benefits, potential pitfalls of procrastination, and practical steps you can take to secure your financial future. So, let's dive in!

❖ **Building a Nest Egg:** Imagine retirement as a journey. The earlier you embark on it, the more resources you'll have to fuel your voyage. Saving early allows your money to grow exponentially through the power of compounding. Compounding is like a snowball effect, where your initial investment earns returns, and those returns, in turn, generate more returns. Starting early gives your investments more time to compound, resulting in a significantly larger nest egg by the time you retire.

- ❖ **Mitigating Financial Risks:** Life is unpredictable, and financial emergencies can arise at any time. Saving for retirement early acts as a safety net, providing you with a cushion to weather unforeseen circumstances. Whether it's a medical emergency, job loss, or economic downturn, having a robust retirement fund offers peace of mind, knowing that you have a financial buffer to rely on during tough times.

- ❖ **Harnessing the Power of Time:** Time is your greatest ally when it comes to saving for retirement. The longer your money stays invested, the more it can grow. By starting early, you can afford to take a more balanced approach to investing, allocating a portion of your portfolio to higher-risk, higher-return investments, such as stocks. Over time, these investments have the potential to deliver significant gains, helping you build a more substantial retirement fund.

- ❖ **Avoiding Catch-Up Contributions:** One common pitfall of delaying retirement savings is the need for catch-up contributions later in life. As retirement approaches, individuals who haven't saved enough may feel compelled to make larger contributions to make up for lost time. However, playing catch-up can be challenging, especially if you're faced with competing financial priorities, such as paying off debt or covering everyday expenses. Starting early eliminates the need for catch-up contributions, allowing you to save gradually over time without feeling the pinch.

Example:

Meet Sarah and Mark, both 30 years old, earning $60,000 annually, and planning for retirement.

Sarah diligently contributes 6% of her salary to her 401(k) plan, taking full advantage of her employer's 50% matching contribution, which amounts to $3,600 per year. Assuming an average annual return of 7% on her investments, Sarah's retirement savings will grow to approximately $869,000 by the time she is 65.

On the other hand, Mark decides not to contribute to a retirement savings plan, believing he can catch up later. He spends his entire salary without saving for retirement. As a result, Mark misses out on the opportunity to benefit from compounding and employer matching contributions.

When Sarah and Mark reach 65, Sarah has a substantial retirement nest egg of $869,000, while Mark has no retirement savings. Sarah's disciplined approach to saving for retirement has paid off, providing her with financial security in retirement, while Mark faces uncertainty and regrets not starting sooner.

This example illustrates the significant impact of saving for retirement early and taking advantage of employer matching contributions. Starting early and making regular contributions can make a substantial difference in the size of your retirement savings, providing you with peace of mind and financial security in your golden years.

In conclusion, saving for retirement early is not just a good idea; it's essential for securing your financial future. By starting early, you can take advantage of compounding, mitigate financial risks, harness the power of time, and avoid the need for catch-up contributions. So, don't wait until tomorrow—start saving today. Your future self will thank you for it.

Remember, retirement may seem distant, but the decisions you make today will shape your tomorrows. By prioritizing saving and making it a habit, you can build a solid foundation for the retirement you envision. So, take that first step towards financial security and start saving for retirement early. Your future self will thank you for it.

1.7.2 Planning for Retirement? Explore Your Options with 401(k)s and IRAs

When it comes to planning for retirement, knowledge is power. Understanding your retirement savings options can help you make informed decisions that pave the way for a financially secure future. In this topic, we'll introduce you to two popular retirement savings vehicles—401(k)s and IRAs. We'll explore how these accounts work, their key features, and how you can make the most of them to build a robust retirement nest egg. So, let's dive in and explore your options!

❖ **401(k) Plans:** A 401(k) is an employer-sponsored retirement savings plan that allows employees to contribute a portion of their pre-tax income to a retirement account. One of the key benefits of a 401(k) is employer matching contributions, where employers match a portion of the employee's contributions, up to a certain percentage. This is essentially free money that can boost your retirement savings.

- ❖ **Traditional IRAs:** Individual Retirement Accounts (IRAs) are another popular retirement savings option. Unlike 401(k)s, which are employer-sponsored, IRAs are individual accounts that anyone with earned income can contribute to. Traditional IRAs offer tax-deferred growth, meaning you won't pay taxes on your contributions or earnings until you withdraw the money in retirement. This can result in significant tax savings over time.

- ❖ **Roth IRAs:** Roth IRAs are another type of IRA that offer tax advantages. Unlike traditional IRAs, contributions to Roth IRAs are made with after-tax dollars, meaning you won't get a tax deduction for your contributions. However, qualified withdrawals from Roth IRAs are tax-free, providing a valuable source of tax-free income in retirement.

- ❖ **Self-Employed Retirement Plans:** If you're self-employed or own a small business, you have several retirement savings options available to you. These include SEP-IRAs, SIMPLE IRAs, and Solo 401(k)s, each with its own contribution limits and tax advantages. These plans can help self-employed individuals save for retirement while taking advantage of tax benefits like those available to employees of larger companies.

Example:

Meet Sarah, a 35-year-old marketing manager who is starting to think seriously about retirement. Sarah has been diligent about saving for retirement and has been contributing to her employer's 401(k) plan for the past ten years. She also opened a Roth IRA five years ago to supplement her retirement savings.

Sarah's 401(k) plan allows her to contribute up to 10% of her salary, and her employer matches 50% of her contributions, up to 6% of her salary. Sarah takes full advantage of this matching contribution, as it's essentially free money that helps boost her retirement savings.

In addition to her 401(k), Sarah contributes $500 per month to her Roth IRA. While she doesn't get a tax deduction for her contributions, she likes the flexibility of being able to withdraw her contributions tax-free at any time, if needed.

Sarah's diligent saving habits have paid off, and she has built a substantial retirement nest egg. She plans to continue saving aggressively for the next 30 years, with the goal of retiring comfortably and enjoying the fruits of her labor.

Sarah's story highlights the importance of understanding your retirement savings options and making informed decisions. By taking advantage of employer-sponsored plans like 401(k)s and individual accounts like IRAs, Sarah has set herself up for a secure financial future in retirement.

In conclusion, understanding your retirement savings options is key to building a secure financial future. 401(k)s and IRAs are powerful tools that can help you save for retirement while taking advantage of tax benefits and employer contributions. By exploring these options and choosing the ones that best suit your financial goals, you can take control of your retirement savings and set yourself up for a comfortable retirement.

So, whether you're just starting your career or nearing retirement age, it's never too early or too late to start saving for retirement. By exploring your options and making informed decisions, you can build a robust retirement nest egg that will provide for you in your golden years.

1.7.3 Boost Your Retirement Savings: The Power of Employer Matching Contributions

Imagine someone offering you free money—would you take it? When it comes to saving for retirement, many employers offer just that through matching contributions to retirement savings plans. In this topic, we'll delve into the concept of employer matching contributions, exploring how they work and the significant benefits they offer to your retirement savings. So, if you're looking to supercharge your retirement savings, read on to discover the power of employer matching contributions!

- ❖ **How Employer Matching Contributions Work:** Employer matching contributions are a benefit offered by many employers as part of their retirement savings plans, such as 401(k)s. When you contribute to your retirement savings plan, your employer will match a portion of your contributions, up to a certain percentage of your salary. For example, if your employer offers a 50% match on contributions up to 6% of your salary and you contribute 6% of your salary, your employer will contribute an additional 3%—effectively doubling your contribution.

- ❖ **Benefits of Employer Matching Contributions:** Taking advantage of employer matching contributions can significantly boost your retirement savings. Not only do these contributions increase the amount of money you're saving for retirement, but they also provide an immediate return on your investment. This is essentially free money that can help you reach your retirement goals faster and more efficiently.

- ❖ **Tax Benefits:** In addition to the immediate benefits of employer matching contributions, there are also long-term tax benefits. Contributions to traditional 401(k) plans are made with pre-tax dollars, meaning you won't pay taxes on your contributions until you withdraw the money in retirement. This can result in significant tax savings over time, allowing your contributions to grow tax-deferred until retirement.

- ❖ **Maximizing Your Employer Match:** To make the most of employer matching contributions, it's important to understand your employer's matching policy and contribute enough to receive the full match. If your employer offers a match, but you're not contributing enough to receive it, you're essentially leaving free money on the table. By maximizing your employer match, you can accelerate your retirement savings and build a more secure financial future.

Example:

Meet Emily, a 30-year-old marketing manager who is eager to start saving for retirement. Emily's employer offers a 401(k) plan with a matching contribution of 50% of employee contributions, up to 6% of her salary.

Emily decides to contribute 6% of her $60,000 annual salary to her 401(k) plan, which amounts to $3,600 per year, or $300 per month. Thanks to her employer's matching contribution, Emily's savings receive an additional $1,800 per year, bringing her total annual contributions to $5,400.

Over the next 35 years, assuming an average annual return of 7% on her investments, Emily's contributions, combined with her employer's matching contributions and the power of compounding, will grow to approximately $869,000. Without her employer's matching contributions, Emily's savings would only amount to $579,000—a difference of $290,000.

By taking advantage of her employer's matching contributions, Emily has been able to significantly boost her retirement savings and set herself up for a more financially secure future. Her story underscores the importance of maximizing employer matching contributions to make the most of your retirement savings.

In conclusion, employer matching contributions are a valuable benefit that can significantly boost your retirement savings. By taking advantage of employer matching contributions, you can increase the amount of money you're saving for retirement, benefit from immediate and long-term tax advantages, and accelerate your path to a secure financial future.

So, if you're not already taking advantage of your employer's matching contributions, now is the time to start. By maximizing your employer match, you can supercharge your retirement savings and set yourself up for a comfortable retirement.

In conclusion, planning for retirement is a crucial step in securing your financial future, and understanding your retirement savings options is key to building a robust retirement nest egg. By exploring options like 401(k)s, IRAs, and employer matching contributions, you can take control of your financial future and set yourself up for a comfortable retirement.

Starting early is essential, as it allows your money to grow through the power of compounding, maximizing your savings potential. Taking advantage of employer matching contributions can significantly boost your retirement savings, providing immediate and long-term benefits that can accelerate your path to financial security.

So, whether you're just starting your career or nearing retirement age, it's never too early or too late to start saving for retirement. By making informed decisions and taking advantage of available options, you can build a solid foundation for the retirement you envision. Your future self will thank you for it.

1.8 Insurance Needs

1.8.1 Understanding the Basics: Types of Insurance Explained

Insurance plays a crucial role in our lives, offering protection and peace of mind against unexpected events. There are several types of insurance, each serving a specific purpose. Understanding these types can help you make informed decisions about your insurance needs. In this topic, we will define and explain some common types of insurance, including health, life, auto, and home insurance.

Imagine this:

It's a typical Monday morning, and Sarah is getting ready for work. As she rushes to leave, she slips on a wet floor in her kitchen and falls, breaking her leg. Unable to work for several weeks, Sarah faces not only medical bills but also a loss of income.

Without health insurance, Sarah would have to pay for her medical expenses out of pocket, which could amount to thousands of dollars. With health insurance, however, Sarah's medical bills are covered, allowing her to focus on her recovery without worrying about the financial burden.

But the challenges don't end there. Sarah's car, which she relies on to get to work, is damaged in an accident on her way to a doctor's appointment. Without auto insurance, Sarah would have to pay for the repairs or a replacement vehicle herself, adding to her financial strain.

Fortunately, Sarah has auto insurance, which covers the cost of repairs to her car. This allows her to get back on the road quickly and continue with her daily activities.

As Sarah reflects on these events, she realizes the importance of insurance in protecting her financial well-being. Whether it's health, auto, or another type of insurance, having the right coverage can make all the difference in times of need.

Sarah's story highlights the importance of insurance in protecting against unexpected events. From medical emergencies to car accidents, insurance provides peace of mind and financial security when it's needed most. By ensuring you have the right insurance coverage for your needs, you can protect yourself and your loved ones from unforeseen circumstances.

Types of Insurance:

1. **Health Insurance**: Health insurance covers medical expenses incurred due to illness, injury, or disability. It helps you pay for medical services, including doctor visits, hospital stays, prescription medications, and

preventive care. Health insurance can be provided by employers, purchased independently, or provided by the government (e.g., Medicare, Medicaid).

2. **Life Insurance**: Life insurance provides financial protection to your loved ones in the event of your death. It pays out a sum of money, known as the death benefit, to your beneficiaries. There are several types of life insurance, including term life, whole life, and universal life, each with its own features and benefits.

3. **Auto Insurance**: Auto insurance provides financial protection against physical damage and bodily injury resulting from traffic collisions and against liability that could also arise from incidents in a vehicle. It is a legal requirement in most states and typically includes coverage for property damage, medical payments, and liability.

4. **Home Insurance**: Home insurance, also known as homeowner's insurance, protects your home and its contents against damage or loss from perils such as fire, theft, vandalism, and natural disasters. It also provides liability coverage in case someone is injured on your property.

In conclusion, insurance is an essential part of financial planning, providing protection against unforeseen events. Health insurance covers medical expenses, life insurance provides financial security to your loved ones, auto insurance protects against vehicle-related risks, and home insurance safeguards your home and belongings. By understanding the types of insurance available, you can make informed decisions to protect yourself and your assets.

1.8.2 The Crucial Shield: Why Adequate Insurance Coverage Is Essential

Introduction: Imagine waking up to find your home flooded or receiving a devastating medical diagnosis without the safety net of insurance. Adequate insurance coverage is more than just a safety precaution; it's a lifeline that protects you from financial ruin in the face of unexpected events. In this topic, we'll explore the importance of having adequate insurance coverage and how it can safeguard your financial well-being.

1. **Protection Against Financial Loss**: Adequate insurance coverage provides protection against financial loss due to unforeseen events. For example, health insurance can help cover medical expenses, while auto insurance can protect you from the financial burden of repairing or replacing your vehicle after an accident. Without insurance, you may be forced to deplete your savings or take on debt to cover these expenses.

2. **Peace of Mind**: Having adequate insurance coverage can provide peace of mind, knowing that you and your loved ones are protected in case of an emergency. For instance, life insurance can ensure that your family is financially secure if something were to happen to you. This peace of mind is invaluable and can help you focus on other aspects of your life without worrying about the financial consequences of a crisis.

3. **Legal Requirements**: In many cases, having insurance coverage is a legal requirement. For example, auto insurance is mandatory in most states to protect other drivers in the event of an accident. Failing to have adequate insurance coverage can result in fines, penalties, and even legal action.

4. **Safeguarding Your Assets**: Insurance coverage can help safeguard your assets, such as your home, car, and personal belongings. For example, home insurance can protect your home and its contents from damage or theft, while renters insurance can protect your belongings if you're renting a property. Without insurance, you could be left with significant financial losses if disaster strikes.

In conclusion, having adequate insurance coverage is essential for protecting yourself and your assets from unforeseen events. Whether it's health, life, auto, or home insurance, having the right coverage can provide financial security and peace of mind. By ensuring that you have adequate insurance coverage, you can rest assured knowing that you're prepared for whatever life throws your way.

1.8.3 Finding Your Shield: Tips for Choosing the Right Insurance Coverage

Choosing the right insurance coverage can be overwhelming, with numerous options available and varying costs to consider. However, finding the right coverage for your individual needs and budget is crucial for protecting yourself and your assets. In this topic, we'll offer tips on how to navigate the world of insurance and find the coverage that's right for you.

1. **Assess Your Needs**: Before you start looking for insurance coverage, take the time to assess your needs. Consider factors such as your health, lifestyle, assets, and financial obligations. For example, if you have a family to support, life insurance may be a priority. Understanding your needs will help you prioritize the types of coverage you require.

2. **Research Different Insurance Options**: Research different types of insurance policies available to determine which ones align with your needs. For example, if you're looking for health insurance, compare different plans based on coverage, premiums, and out-of-pocket costs. Consider consulting with an insurance agent or broker to get expert advice on the best options for you.

3. **Compare Quotes:** Once you've identified the types of coverage you need, shop around and compare quotes from multiple insurance providers. Look for policies that offer the coverage you need at a price that fits your budget. Be sure to consider factors such as deductibles, coverage limits, and exclusions when comparing quotes.

4. **Review Policy Details Carefully**: Before committing to an insurance policy, review the policy details carefully. Pay attention to the coverage limits, exclusions, and any additional benefits or features offered. Make sure you understand what is and isn't covered by the policy to avoid any surprises later on.

5. **Consider Bundling Policies**: Many insurance providers offer discounts for bundling multiple policies, such as auto and home insurance. Consider bundling

your policies with the same provider to save money on premiums.

Finding the right insurance coverage for your individual needs and budget requires careful consideration and research. By assessing your needs, researching different options, comparing quotes, reviewing policy details, and considering bundling policies, you can find the coverage that offers the protection you need at a price you can afford.

Meet John, a young professional looking to secure the right insurance coverage for his needs and budget. Let's follow John as he explores different insurance options and applies our tips to find the best coverage for him.

1. **Assessing Needs:** John starts by assessing his needs. He is single, healthy, and has no dependents. He decides that health insurance is his top priority, followed by renter's insurance to protect his belongings. Life insurance is not a priority for him at this stage of his life.

2. **Researching Options:** John reviews the health insurance options offered by his employer. John researches different health insurance plans and finds two options: Plan A and Plan B. Plan A has a lower premium but higher out-of-pocket costs, while Plan B has a higher premium but lower out-of-pocket costs. For renter's insurance, John compares quotes from different providers to find the most affordable option.

3. **Comparing Quotes:** For health insurance, John compares the monthly premiums and out-of-pocket costs for both Plan A and Plan B. Plan A has a monthly premium of $200 and an annual deductible of $3,000, while Plan B has a monthly premium of $300 and an annual deductible of $1,500. For renter's insurance, John receives quotes ranging from $10 to $20 per month.

4. **Reviewing Policy Details:** John carefully reviews the policy details for both health insurance plans to understand the coverage limits, exclusions, and additional benefits. He also reviews the coverage limits and exclusions for the renter's insurance quotes to ensure they meet his needs.

5. **Considering Bundling Policies:** John considers bundling his health and renter's insurance policies with the same provider to save money on premiums. After comparing the bundled quote with individual quotes, he decides that bundling is a cost-effective option for him.

By following these tips, John was able to find the right insurance coverage for his needs and budget. He chose Plan B for health insurance due to its lower out-of-pocket costs, and he opted to bundle his health and renter's insurance policies for additional savings. John's example demonstrates how careful consideration and research can help you find the best insurance coverage for your individual circumstances.

Navigating the world of insurance can be complex, but with the right approach, you can find the coverage that meets your needs and fits your budget. Start by assessing your needs and researching different insurance options. Compare quotes, review policy details carefully, and consider bundling policies to save money. Whether you're looking for health, life, auto, home, or employer-provided insurance, taking the time to find the right coverage can provide you with peace of mind and financial security in the face of life's uncertainties. By following these tips, you can make informed decisions and ensure that you have the protection you need when you need it most.

1.9 Estate Planning

1.9.1 Understanding Estate Planning and Its Importance in Fulfilling Your Wishes After You're Gone

Have you ever thought about what happens to your assets, property, and belongings after you pass away? Estate planning is a crucial step in ensuring that your wishes are carried out after death. In this topic, we will delve into the definition of estate planning, its importance, and how it can help you protect your legacy and provide for your loved ones. So, let's explore this essential aspect of financial planning together.

Estate planning is the process of arranging for the management and disposal of a person's estate during their life and after death. It involves making decisions about who will inherit your assets, who will manage your affairs if you become incapacitated, and how your debts will be paid. Estate planning is not just for the wealthy; it is for anyone who wants to ensure that their wishes are carried out and their loved ones are provided for after they are gone.

1. **Understanding the Components of Estate Planning**

  - ➤ Wills and Trusts: A will is a legal document that specifies how your assets will be distributed after your death. A trust is a legal arrangement where a trustee holds assets on behalf of beneficiaries.

  - ➤ Power of Attorney: This document allows you to appoint someone to make financial or medical decisions on your behalf if you become unable to do so.

  - ➤ Advance Directive: Also known as a living will, this document outlines your wishes regarding medical treatment if you are unable to communicate them yourself.

2. **Importance of Estate Planning**

  - ➤ Ensures Your Wishes Are Carried Out: Estate planning allows you to specify how you want your assets to be distributed and who will manage your affairs after you're gone.

  - ➤ Minimizes Family Disputes: Clear estate planning can help avoid misunderstandings and conflicts among family members regarding asset distribution.

  - ➤ Provides for Your Loved Ones: Estate planning ensures that your loved ones are provided for financially, especially if they rely on you for support.

  - ➤ Reduces Tax Burden: Proper estate planning can help minimize estate taxes, leaving more of your assets to your beneficiaries.

3. **Example: Importance of Estate Planning**

> ➢ Consider a scenario where a person passes away without a will. Their assets will be distributed according to the state's intestacy laws, which may not align with their wishes. This can lead to family disputes and financial hardships for loved ones.

In conclusion, estate planning is a crucial step in ensuring that your wishes are carried out after your death. By taking the time to create a comprehensive estate plan, you can protect your legacy, provide for your loved ones, and minimize the potential for family disputes. So, don't wait until it's too late. Start planning your estate today to secure a better tomorrow for your loved ones.

Example:

Meet Sarah, a 45-year-old single mother of two teenage children, Emily and Jack. Sarah has worked hard her entire life to provide for her family and ensure they have a comfortable life. However, Sarah has never gotten around to creating an estate plan because she thought it was something only wealthy people needed.

Tragically, Sarah unexpectedly passes away in a car accident, leaving Emily and Jack devastated and unsure about what to do next. Since Sarah never created a will or designated a guardian for her children, the court must step in to make these decisions. Emily and Jack are placed in the care of a distant relative whom Sarah would not have chosen.

Furthermore, Sarah's assets, including her house and savings, are distributed according to state law, which may not align with her wishes. As a result, Emily and Jack face financial uncertainty, and there is a potential for disputes among family members over Sarah's estate.

If Sarah had taken the time to create an estate plan, she could have specified who would care for her children, how her assets should be distributed, and ensured that her wishes were carried out. Estate planning would have provided peace of mind for Sarah and her children, knowing that their future was secure.

Sarah's story highlights the importance of estate planning for everyone, regardless of their financial situation. It's not just about protecting assets; it's about ensuring that your loved ones are provided for and that your wishes are carried out after you're gone.

1.9.2 Understanding the Key Components of an Estate Plan: Wills, Powers of Attorney, and Healthcare Directives

Have you ever wondered what documents make up an estate plan and how they can protect you and your loved ones? In this topic, we will explore the essential components of an estate plan, including wills, powers of attorney, and healthcare directives. Understanding these components is crucial for ensuring that your wishes are carried out and your loved ones are provided for in the future. So, let's dive into the world of estate planning together.

An estate plan is a set of legal documents that outline how you want your assets to be managed and distributed after your death. It also includes documents that specify who will make decisions on your behalf if you become incapacitated. Three key components of an estate plan are wills, powers of attorney, and healthcare directives. These documents are essential for ensuring that your wishes are carried out and that your loved ones are taken care of.

1. **Wills**

   - A will is a legal document that specifies how your assets will be distributed after your death.

   - It allows you to name an executor who will be responsible for carrying out your wishes.

   - A will can also include provisions for guardianship of minor children and the distribution of personal belongings.

   - Example: Sarah's will specifies that her house will be left to her daughter Emily and her savings will be divided equally between Emily and her son Jack.

2. **Powers of Attorney**

   - A power of attorney is a legal document that allows you to appoint someone to make financial or medical decisions on your behalf if you become unable to do so.

   - There are two types of powers of attorney: financial power of attorney and medical power of attorney.

   - Example: Sarah appoints her sister as her financial power of attorney to manage her finances if she becomes incapacitated.

3. **Healthcare Directives**

> ➢ A healthcare directive, also known as a living will, is a document that outlines your wishes regarding medical treatment if you are unable to communicate them yourself.

> ➢ It can specify the type of medical care you do or do not want to receive.

> ➢ Example: Sarah's healthcare directive states that she does not want to be kept on life support if there is no chance of recovery.

In conclusion, wills, powers of attorney, and healthcare directives are essential components of an estate plan. They allow you to specify how you want your assets to be distributed, who will make decisions on your behalf if you become incapacitated, and what medical care you do or do not want to receive. By taking the time to create these documents, you can ensure that your wishes are carried out and that your loved ones are provided for according to your wishes.

1.9.3 Essential Tips for Creating and Maintaining an Effective Estate Plan

Creating an estate plan is a crucial step in ensuring that your wishes are carried out and your loved ones are provided for after you're gone. However, it's not enough to create an estate plan once and forget about it. It's essential to review and update your plan regularly to reflect any changes in your life or finances. In this topic, we will discuss some tips for creating an effective estate plan and keeping it up to date. By following these tips, you can ensure that your estate plan remains relevant and effective throughout your life.

Creating an estate plan is a vital part of financial planning. It involves making decisions about how your assets will be distributed after your death and who will make decisions on your behalf if you become incapacitated. However, creating an estate plan is not a one-time task. It's important to review and update your plan regularly to ensure that it reflects your current wishes and circumstances.

1. **Start Early and Review Regularly**

   - It's never too early to start planning your estate. The sooner you start, the more time you have to make decisions and ensure that your wishes are carried out.

   - Review your estate plan regularly, especially after major life events such as marriage, divorce, birth of a child, or significant changes in your financial situation.

2. **Work with a Professional**

   - Consider working with an estate planning attorney to help you create a comprehensive estate plan that meets your specific needs and goals.

   - A professional can help you navigate the complexities of estate planning and ensure that your plan complies with state laws.

3. **Consider All Aspects of Your Estate**

   - Your estate plan should include more than just a will. Consider including powers of attorney, healthcare directives, and trusts to ensure that all aspects of your estate are covered.

> Think about how you want your assets to be distributed, who will make decisions on your behalf if you become incapacitated, and what medical care you do or do not want to receive.

4. Communicate Your Wishes

> Communicate your wishes to your loved ones and the individuals you have appointed to make decisions on your behalf.

> Ensure that your loved ones know where to find your estate planning documents and how to access them when the time comes.

In conclusion, creating an estate plan is an essential part of financial planning. By starting early, working with a professional, considering all aspects of your estate, and communicating your wishes, you can create an effective estate plan that reflects your wishes and provides for your loved ones. Remember to review and update your plan regularly to ensure that it remains relevant and effective throughout your life.

1.9.4 Examples of Wills and How to Create One

A will is a crucial legal document that outlines your wishes regarding the distribution of your assets and the care of any minor children after your death. Here are some examples of wills and how you can create one to ensure your wishes are carried out.

Example 1: Simple Will

"I, [Your Name], being of sound mind, declare this to be my Last Will and Testament. I revoke all prior wills and codicils. I appoint [Executor's Name] as the executor of my estate. I direct that my debts, funeral expenses, and estate administration expenses be paid as soon as practicable after my death.

I give, devise, and bequeath all of my estate, both real and personal, of whatsoever nature and wheresoever situated, to my spouse, [Spouse's Name], if [he/she] survives me; otherwise, to my children, [Child 1's Name] and [Child 2's Name], in equal shares, per stirpes.

I direct that if any beneficiary under this will contests this will or any of its provisions, then that beneficiary shall forfeit any share or interest in my estate."

Example 2: Will with Trusts for Minor Children

"I, [Your Name], being of sound mind, declare this to be my Last Will and Testament. I appoint [Executor's Name] as the executor of my estate. I direct that my debts, funeral expenses, and estate administration expenses be paid as soon as practicable after my death.

I give, devise, and bequeath all of my estate, both real and personal, of whatsoever nature and wheresoever situated, to my spouse, [Spouse's Name], if [he/she] survives me; otherwise, to a trust for the benefit of my minor children, [Child 1's Name] and [Child 2's Name].

I direct that the trustee of the trust shall distribute the income and principal of the trust for the benefit of my minor children, as the trustee deems necessary for their health, education, maintenance, and support, until they reach the age of [Age of Majority].

I appoint [Trustee's Name] as the trustee of the trust and authorize the trustee to invest and reinvest the trust property in such manner as the trustee deems advisable."

How to Create a Will

1. **Decide on Your Beneficiaries**: Determine who will receive your assets after your death.

2. **Appoint an Executor**: Choose someone you trust to manage your estate and carry out your wishes.

3. **List Your Assets**: Make a list of all your assets, including bank accounts, real estate, investments, and personal belongings.

4. **Draft Your Will**: You can draft your will yourself using a template or online service, or you can hire an estate planning attorney to help you.

5. **Sign Your Will**: Your will must be signed in the presence of witnesses to be legally valid. Check your state's requirements for the number of witnesses needed.

6. **Store Your Will Safely**: Keep your will in a safe place, such as a safe deposit box, and let your executor know where it is located.

7. **Review and Update Your Will**: Regularly review your will and update it as needed to reflect any changes in your life or wishes.

Creating a will is an important step in ensuring that your wishes are carried out after your death. By following these steps and examples, you can create a comprehensive will that provides for your loved ones and protects your legacy.

1.9.5 Example of Power of Attorney and How to Create One

A power of attorney is a legal document that allows you to appoint someone to make financial or medical decisions on your behalf if you become unable to do so. Here is an example of a power of attorney and how you can create one to ensure your affairs are managed according to your wishes.

Example of Financial Power of Attorney

"I, [Your Name], appoint [Agent's Name] as my attorney-in-fact to act on my behalf in all matters relating to my financial affairs. This includes, but is not limited to, managing my bank accounts, paying bills, buying or selling property, and handling tax matters.

This power of attorney shall become effective immediately and shall remain in effect until revoked by me in writing. I authorize my attorney-in-fact to act on my behalf and to sign any documents necessary to carry out the powers granted in this document.

I certify that I am of sound mind and that I am executing this power of attorney voluntarily and without undue influence."

How to Create a Power of Attorney

1. **Choose Your Agent**: Select someone you trust to act as your attorney-in-fact. This could be a family member, friend, or professional advisor.

2. **Decide on the Powers**: Determine the scope of the powers you want to grant to your attorney-in-fact. You can grant broad powers or limit them to specific tasks.

3. **Draft the Power of Attorney**: You can create a power of attorney yourself using a template or online service, or you can seek the assistance of an attorney.

4. **Sign the Power of Attorney**: You must sign the power of attorney in the presence of a notary public to make it legally valid.

5. **Provide a Copy to Your Agent**: Give a copy of the power of attorney to your attorney-in-fact and any institutions or individuals who may need to recognize it.

6. **Review and Update as Needed**: Regularly review your power of attorney and update it as needed to reflect any changes in your circumstances or wishes.

Creating a power of attorney is an important step in ensuring that your affairs are managed according to your wishes if you become unable to do so yourself. By following these steps and example, you can create a power of attorney that provides you with peace of mind knowing that your financial affairs are in good hands.

1.9.6 Example of Healthcare Directive and How to Create One

A healthcare directive, also known as a living will, is a legal document that outlines your wishes regarding medical treatment if you are unable to communicate them yourself. Here is an example of a healthcare directive and how you can create one to ensure your medical wishes are followed.

Example of Healthcare Directive

"I, [Your Name], being of sound mind, hereby declare this to be my healthcare directive. If I am unable to make healthcare decisions for myself, I direct that:

1. If I am in a terminal condition and there is no reasonable expectation of my recovery, I do not want life-prolonging procedures to be used.

2. If I am in a persistent vegetative state and there is no reasonable expectation of my recovery, I do not want life-prolonging procedures to be used.

3. If I am unable to feed myself, I do not want artificial nutrition or hydration to be used.

I appoint [Agent's Name] as my healthcare agent to make healthcare decisions for me if I am unable to do so. I authorize my healthcare agent to make decisions on my behalf, including the withholding or withdrawal of life-prolonging procedures.

I understand the full import of this directive and I am emotionally and mentally competent to make this directive."

How to Create a Healthcare Directive

1. **Determine Your Wishes**: Think about the medical treatments you would want or not want if you were unable to communicate your wishes. Consider discussing your wishes with your healthcare provider and loved ones.

2. **Draft the Directive**: You can create a healthcare directive yourself using a template or online service, or you can seek the assistance of an attorney.

3. **Sign the Directive**: You must sign the healthcare directive in the presence of witnesses to make it legally valid. Check your state's requirements for the number of witnesses needed.

4. **Provide Copies to Relevant Parties**: Give copies of your healthcare directive to your healthcare provider, healthcare agent, and loved ones. Ensure that they understand your wishes and know where to find the document if needed.

5. **Review and Update as Needed**: Regularly review your healthcare directive and update it as needed to reflect any changes in your circumstances or wishes.

Creating a healthcare directive is an important step in ensuring that your medical wishes are followed if you are unable to communicate them yourself. By following these steps and example, you can create a healthcare directive that provides you with peace of mind knowing that your healthcare decisions will be respected.

1.10 Financial Planning Tools

1.10.1 Introducing Tools and Resources for Financial Planning

In today's fast-paced world, managing your finances effectively is more important than ever. Thankfully, numerous tools and resources are available to help you achieve your financial goals. From budgeting apps that track your spending to retirement calculators that estimate your future needs, and investment platforms that enable you to grow your wealth, these resources can make financial planning accessible and even enjoyable.

1. **Budgeting Apps:** Budgeting apps like Mint and You Need A Budget (YNAB) have revolutionized how people manage their finances. Mint, for example, categorizes your spending, tracks your bills, and provides insights into your financial habits. YNAB takes a proactive approach, emphasizing the importance of giving every dollar a job and helping you break the paycheck-to-paycheck cycle.

2. **Retirement Calculators:** Planning for retirement can be daunting, but retirement calculators simplify the process. These tools consider factors like your current age, desired retirement age, life expectancy, and savings rate to estimate how much you need to save each month to reach your retirement goals. Examples include calculators from Fidelity, Vanguard, and T. Rowe Price.

3. **Investment Platforms:** Investing is crucial for building wealth, and platforms like Robinhood and Vanguard make it accessible to everyone. Robinhood offers commission-free trading of stocks, ETFs, options, and cryptocurrencies, making it ideal for beginners. Vanguard, on the other hand, is known for its low-cost index funds and ETFs, making it a favorite among long-term investors.

In conclusion, the key to successful financial planning is using the right tools and resources. Budgeting apps, retirement calculators, and investment platforms can simplify complex financial concepts, empower you to make informed decisions, and ultimately help you achieve financial freedom. So, take advantage of these tools and start planning for a brighter financial future today.

Link: Get your first up to $200 Stock **- Sign up Now**

Robinhood has revolutionized the world of investing by offering commission-free trading of stocks, ETFs, options, and cryptocurrencies. Here are some of the key features and benefits of using Robinhood:

Features:

1. **Commission-Free Trading:** Robinhood allows users to trade stocks, ETFs, options, and cryptocurrencies without paying any commission fees. This makes it an attractive option for investors looking to minimize costs.

2. **Fractional Shares:** Robinhood offers the ability to purchase fractional shares of stocks and ETFs, allowing investors to buy into high-priced stocks with as little as $1.

3. **Simple and Intuitive Interface:** Robinhood's app features a simple and intuitive interface, making it easy

for users to buy and sell investments, track their portfolio, and access market news and analysis.

4. **Cash Management:** Robinhood offers a cash management feature that allows users to earn interest on uninvested cash in their account. Users can also use the feature to pay bills, make purchases, and withdraw cash from ATMs.

5. **Robinhood Gold:** Robinhood Gold is a premium subscription service that offers additional features, such as extended trading hours, access to professional research reports, and the ability to trade on margin.

Benefits:

1. **Cost-Effective:** Robinhood's commission-free trading model makes it a cost-effective option for investors, especially those who trade frequently or with small amounts of money.

2. **Accessible:** Robinhood's low minimum investment requirements and fractional shares make investing accessible to a wider range of people, including those with limited funds.

3. **Educational Resources:** Robinhood offers educational resources, such as topics and videos, to help investors learn more about investing and make informed decisions.

4. **Convenience:** Robinhood's mobile app allows investors to manage their investments from anywhere, making it convenient for busy individuals.

5. **Diverse Investment Options:** Robinhood offers a wide range of investment options, including stocks, ETFs,

options, and cryptocurrencies, allowing investors to build a diverse portfolio.

In conclusion, Robinhood offers a range of features and benefits that make it an attractive option for investors looking to manage their investments effectively. Whether you're a beginner looking to get started with investing or an experienced investor looking to minimize costs, Robinhood has something to offer.

Mint

Link: Mint

Mint is a popular budgeting app that offers a wide range of features to help users track their spending, manage their budgets, and achieve their financial goals. Here are some of the key features and benefits of using Mint:

Features:

1. **Budgeting:** Mint allows users to create custom budgets based on their income and expenses. The app automatically categorizes transactions and compares them to the budget, providing real-time updates on spending habits.

2. **Transaction Tracking:** Users can link their bank accounts, credit cards, and other financial accounts to Mint, allowing the app to track transactions automatically. This feature helps users stay on top of their finances and identify any unusual or unauthorized transactions.

3. **Bill Payment Reminders:** Mint can send reminders for upcoming bill payments, helping users avoid late fees and missed payments. Users can also set up automatic bill payments directly from the app.

4. **Credit Score Monitoring:** Mint provides users with access to their credit scores for free. It also offers tips and suggestions for improving credit scores over time.

5. **Goal Setting:** Users can set financial goals, such as saving for a vacation or paying off debt, and track their progress within the app. Mint provides insights and recommendations to help users reach their goals faster.

6. **Investment Tracking:** Mint can track the performance of investment accounts and provide insights into asset allocation and portfolio diversification.

Benefits:

1. **Saves Time:** By automatically tracking transactions and categorizing expenses, Mint saves users time compared to manual budgeting methods.

2. **Promotes Financial Awareness:** Mint's budgeting tools and insights help users understand their spending habits and make informed financial decisions.

3. **Encourages Saving:** The goal-setting feature encourages users to save money for specific goals, helping them build healthy financial habits.

4. **Improves Credit Health:** By monitoring credit scores and providing tips for improvement, Mint helps users maintain or improve their credit health over time.

5. **Customizable:** Mint allows users to customize their budgets and financial goals based on their individual needs and priorities.

In conclusion, Mint is a comprehensive budgeting tool that offers a range of features to help users manage their finances effectively. Whether you're looking to track your spending, save for the future, or improve your credit health, Mint can help you achieve your financial goals.

Link: You Need A Budget (YNAB)

You Need A Budget (YNAB) is a budgeting app that takes a unique approach to financial management, focusing on giving every dollar a job. Here are some of the key features and benefits of using YNAB:

Features:

1. **Zero-Based Budgeting:** YNAB uses zero-based budgeting, which means every dollar is allocated to a specific category, such as groceries, rent, or savings. This approach helps users prioritize their spending and avoid overspending.

2. **Real-Time Syncing:** YNAB syncs with users' bank accounts, credit cards, and other financial accounts in real-time, allowing them to see their updated financial picture at a glance.

3. **Goal Tracking:** Users can set financial goals, such as saving for a vacation or paying off debt, and track their progress within the app. YNAB provides insights and recommendations to help users stay on track.

4. **Debt Paydown Tools:** YNAB offers tools to help users pay down debt faster, such as the Debt Paydown Calculator, which shows the impact of making extra payments towards debt.

5. **Reporting and Insights:** YNAB provides detailed reports and insights into users' spending habits, helping them identify areas where they can cut back and save money.

6. **Mobile Apps:** YNAB offers mobile apps for iOS and Android devices, allowing users to manage their budgets on the go.

Benefits:

1. **Eliminates Financial Stress:** By giving every dollar a job and helping users prioritize their spending, YNAB eliminates the stress of living paycheck to paycheck.

2. **Encourages Savings:** YNAB's goal-setting feature encourages users to save money for specific goals, helping them build healthy financial habits.

3. **Improves Financial Awareness:** YNAB's budgeting tools and insights help users understand their spending habits and make informed financial decisions.

4. **Promotes Accountability:** YNAB's zero-based budgeting approach promotes accountability by requiring users to actively allocate their money to different categories.

5. **Supports Financial Goals:** Whether users are looking to pay off debt, save for the future, or simply gain control over their finances, YNAB can help them achieve their financial goals.

In conclusion, You Need A Budget (YNAB) is a powerful budgeting tool that offers a unique approach to financial management. By giving every dollar a job and helping users prioritize their spending, YNAB can help them achieve financial freedom and peace of mind.

Fidelity

Planning for retirement can be overwhelming, but retirement calculators offer a simple solution. These tools take into account various factors like your age, desired retirement age, life expectancy, and savings rate to estimate how much you need to save each month to reach your retirement goals.

Fidelity Retirement Calculator: Fidelity offers a retirement calculator that takes a comprehensive approach to retirement planning. It considers factors like your current savings, expected Social Security benefits, and desired retirement lifestyle to provide a personalized savings goal. For example, if you're 35 years old, earning $60,000 per year, and want to retire at 65 with an annual income of $50,000, the calculator will estimate how much you need to save each month to achieve this goal.

Link: Fidelity Retirement Calculator

Vanguard

Vanguard Retirement Income Calculator: Vanguard's retirement income calculator focuses on estimating how much income you'll need in retirement and whether your current savings plan is on track to meet that goal. It considers factors like your current savings, expected

retirement age, life expectancy, and investment strategy.
For instance, if you're 45 years old, with $200,000 in
retirement savings, and plan to retire at 65, the calculator
will estimate your monthly retirement income based on
your savings rate and investment returns.

Link: Vanguard Income Calculator

T.Rowe Price

T. Rowe Price Retirement Calculator: T. Rowe Price
offers a retirement calculator that provides a detailed
analysis of your retirement savings goals. It takes into
account factors like your current age, desired retirement
age, annual income, current savings, and expected rate of
return. For example, if you're 50 years old, earning $75,000
per year, and want to retire at 65 with $1 million in savings,
the calculator will estimate how much you need to save
each month to achieve this goal.

Link: T. Rowe Price Retirement Calculator

Retirement calculators are powerful tools that can help you plan for a financially secure retirement. By considering various factors like your age, income, and savings rate, these calculators provide personalized savings goals and actionable insights. Whether you're just starting your career or nearing retirement age, using a retirement calculator can help you make informed decisions and achieve your retirement goals.

Conclusion:

In 'Money Matters 101 - Financial Planning Essentials for Beginners,' we've embarked on a journey to demystify the world of finance, making it accessible to all. From understanding budgeting basics to exploring the intricacies of investing, we've covered a wide array of topics crucial for building a strong financial foundation.

As we conclude this series, remember that financial planning is not just about numbers; it's about creating a secure future and achieving your dreams. By implementing the strategies and tips shared in this book, you'll be better equipped to navigate your financial journey with confidence.

I hope this book has empowered you to take control of your finances and inspired you to embark on a path of lifelong learning and financial prosperity. Remember, the key to financial success lies in education, discipline, and perseverance. Here's to a future filled with financial freedom and security for everyone!"

Upcoming Books:

- **Frugal Living 101: Smart Ways to Save Money**
- Investing 101: Simple Strategies for Wealth Building